Management Guidelines for IUCN Category V Protected Areas Protected Landscapes/Seascapes

IUCN – The World Conservation Union

Founded in 1948, The World Conservation Union brings together States, government agencies and a diverse range of non-governmental organizations in a unique world partnership: over 900 members in all, spread across some 138 countries.

As a Union, IUCN seeks to influence, encourage and assist societies throughout the world to conserve the integrity and diversity of nature and to ensure that any use of natural resources is equitable and ecologically sustainable. A central secretariat co-ordinates the IUCN Programme and serves the Union membership, representing their views on the world stage and providing them with the strategies, services, scientific knowledge and technical support they need to achieve their goals. Through its six Commissions, IUCN draws together over 10,000 expert volunteers in project teams and action groups, focusing in particular on species and biodiversity conservation and the management of habitats and natural resources. The Union has helped many countries to prepare National Conservation Strategies, and demonstrates the application of its know-ledge through the field projects it supervises. Operations are increasingly decentralized and are carried forward by an expanding network of regional and country offices, located principally in developing countries.

The World Conservation Union builds on the strengths of its members, networks and partners to enhance their capacity and to support global alliances to safeguard natural resources at local, regional and global levels.

Cardiff University

The Department of City and Regional Planning, Cardiff University is pleased to be a partner in the production of this important series of guidelines for protected area planning and management. The Department, through its Environmental Planning Research Unit, is actively involved in protected areas research; runs specialised courses on planning and environmental policy; and has a large Graduate School offering opportunities for persons interested in pursuing research for a PhD or as part of wider career development. If you are interested in learning more about the Department, its research capabilities and courses please write to us at the address given below.

Professor Terry Marsden BAHon., PhD, MRTPI
Head of Department
Department of City and Regional Planning
Cardiff University
Glamorgan Building
King Edward VIIth Avenue
Cardiff, CF10 3WA, Wales, UK

Tel: + 44 2920 874022
Fax: + 44 2920 874845
E-mail: MarsdenTK@cf.ac.uk
Web site: www.cf.ac.uk

Management Guidelines for IUCN Category V Protected Areas Protected Landscapes/Seascapes

Adrian Phillips, Author and Series Editor

World Commission on Protected Areas (WCPA)

Best Practice Protected Area Guidelines Series No. 9

IUCN – The World Conservation Union
2002

This publication has been made possible in large part by funding from Cardiff University, the Countryside Agency and IUCN.

Published by: IUCN, Gland, Switzerland, and Cambridge, UK

IUCN
The World Conservation Union

Citation: Phillips, Adrian, (2002). *Management Guidelines for IUCN Category V Protected Areas: Protected Landscapes/Seascapes.* IUCN Gland, Switzerland and Cambridge, UK. xv + 122pp.

ISBN: 2-8317-0685-8

Cover design: IUCN Publications Services Unit

Cover photos: Front: Rice terraces of the Central Cordilleras, Philippines ©*Adrian Phillips*

Back: Poplar grove in Mongolia ©*Sabine Schmidt*; Ilha Comprida, Brazil – boats ©*Marilia Britto de Moraes*; Parco Naturale dell'Argentera, Italy – upland sheep ©*EUROPARC Federation*; Cilento, Italy – rock carving ©*Adrian Phillips*

Layout by: IUCN Publications Services Unit

Produced by: IUCN Publications Services Unit

Printed by: Thanet Press Limited, UK

Available from: IUCN Publications Services Unit
219c Huntingdon Road, Cambridge CB3 0DL,
United Kingdom
Tel: +44 1223 277894
Fax: +44 1223 277175
E-mail: books@iucn.org
www.iucn.org/bookstore

A catalogue of IUCN publications is also available

The text of this book is printed on 90gsm Fineblade Extra made from low-chlorine pulp.

Table of Contents

List of case studies

List of figures

Colour plates   between pages 56–57

Dedication – in memory of PHC (Bing) Lucas

This publication is dedicated to the memory of the late Bing Lucas, who died in December 2000. Bing was widely known, and was held in great affection and deep respect for his work on protected areas around the world. It is less well known that he was an enthusiastic advocate of Protected Landscapes, believing this approach was especially relevant to the conservation and sustainable development needs of our time. He supported and encouraged individuals, institutions and initiatives in this field. He was the author of the first published guidance on the topic in 1992 and keenly supported the decision to revise and update it, which has culminated in this publication. It was written in admiration of his leadership and it is hoped that the result is worthy of his inspiration.

Acknowledgements

IUCN and Cardiff University are indebted to the Countryside Agency, UK, which has supported the production of this publication.

This work was undertaken as part of the programme of the Protected Landscapes Task Force of IUCN's World Commission on Protected Areas (WCPA). More specifically, it was drafted with the guidance of a small core group drawn from the Task Force. The principal author was Adrian Phillips, and the members of the core group were Mike Beresford, Jessica Brown, Prabhu Budhathoki, Brent Mitchell, Peter Ogden, Guillermo Rodriguez, Giles Romulus and Bob Wishitemi. Other members of the Task Force were Marilia Britto de Moraes, Susan Buggey, Mirek Kundrata, Nora Mitchell, Richard Partington, Fausto O. Sarmiento and Guy Swinnerton, all of whom were invited to comment on the draft and several of whom provided case studies. Case studies were also kindly provided by the following: Alejandro Argumedo (Indigenous Peoples' Biodiversity Network), Kevin Bishop (Cardiff University), Sabine Schmidt (GTZ, Mongolia) and Sue Stolton (Equilibrium). Mike Beresford was the main author of Annex 2.

Others who kindly commented on the text, or helped in other ways, include Peter Bridgewater (UNESCO); Anne Drost (QLF/Atlantic Center for the Environment); Vicki Elcoate (UK Council for National Parks); Phil Huffman; Ashish Kothari (Indian Institute for Public Administration); Kishore Rao (IUCN, Vietnam); Pedro Rosabal (IUCN Programme on Protected Areas); Mechtild Rossler (UNESCO World Heritage Centre); Jeff Sayer (WWF International); Zoltán Szilassy (Ministry for Environment and Regional Policy, Hungary); Stephanie Tuxill (QLF/Atlantic Center for the Environment) and Tomme Young (IUCN Environmental Law Centre, Bonn, Germany).

Finally, our thanks go to Yolanda Kakabadse, IUCN President, for her supportive Preface.

Photographs were provided by Marilia Britto de Moraes, EUROPARC Federation, Hortobágy National Park, Brent Mitchell, Niagara Escarpment Commission, Adrian Phillips, Sabine Schmidt, Martin Schneider-Jacoby, Rosie Simpson, Guy Swinnerton and Ken Taylor.

Abbreviations and acronyms

APA	Area de Proteçao Ambiental (Brazil)
AWF	Africa Wildlife Foundation
BZ	Buffer Zone
BZDC	Buffer Zone Development Council (Nepal)
CAP	Common Agricultural Policy (of the EU)
CBD	Convention on Biological Diversity
EIA	Environmental Impact Assessment
ELC	European Landscape Convention
EPOPA	Export Promotion of Organic Products from Africa Programme
EUROPARC Federation	formerly the Federation of Nature and National Parks of Europe
FAO	Food and Agriculture Organization
EA	Environmental Assessment
EU	European Union
FPSN	The Fundación Pro-Sierra Nevada de Santa Marta (Colombia)
FWAG	Farming and Wildlife Advisory Group (UK)
FSC	Forest Stewardship Council
GGSNP	Gobi Gurvan Saikhan National Park (Mongolia)
ICOMOS	International Council on Monuments and Sites
ICEPA	Ilha Comprida Environmental Protection Area (Brazil)
IUCN	The World Conservation Union
LPA	Local Planning Authority (UK)
MSC	Marine Stewardship Council
NCC	National Capital Commission (Canada)
NGO	Non-governmental organisation
NPA	National Park Authority (UK)
RCNP	Royal Chitwan National Park (Nepal)
RDR	Rural Development Regulation (of the EU)
SIDS	Small Island Developing States
SNUC	National System of Conservation Units (Brazil)

SPBCP	South Pacific Biodiversity Conservation Programme
SPREP	South Pacific Regional Environmental Programme
UN	United Nations
UNDP	United Nations Development Programme
UNEP-WCMC	United Nations Environment Programme World Conservation Monitoring Centre
UNESCO	United Nations Educational, Scientific and Cultural Organisation
WCPA	The World Commission on Protected Areas (of IUCN)
WHO	World Health Organisation
WWF	Worldwide Fund for Nature (World Wildlife Fund in North America)

Preface

IUCN has been at the forefront of international work on protected areas for fifty years or so. It has been a leader in the field, a standard setter and a source of professional expertise. Above all, it has been a tireless advocate of the idea that some places in our ever more crowded world should be left inviolate – to meet the needs of people and of nature.

The need to make sure that some places remain in broadly their natural condition is as great as ever – but it is not enough. Protected areas should also include those lived-in, humanised landscapes where people and nature live in some kind of balance. These places, and the communities that live in them, are important in themselves and for the lessons they can teach all of us about sustainable living. This is the idea behind Protected Landscapes and Seascapes, or Category V in the IUCN system of protected area categorisation.

The Category V approach is not a soft option: managing the interface between people and nature is just about the toughest challenge facing society, and Category V management is all about that. Nor are such places second class protected areas: rather they are an essential complement to more strictly protected ones. Indeed, Protected Landscapes are an idea whose time has come, and IUCN is pleased to promote their wider use and higher management standards.

At the Vth World Parks Congress, Durban, South Africa, September 2003, the world's conservation leaders will review the achievements of protected areas over the past ten years and the colossal challenges that face them in future. These call for new approaches and novel ways of working with human societies around the world if we are to conserve the best of the remaining areas of wild nature, and the best of our lived-in landscapes as well. I expect the Category V approach to be a key factor in this strategy.

Which is why I welcome the work of WCPA's Category V Task Force in preparing these guidelines on how to manage such areas, one of several planned outputs from this group before Durban. I am delighted that this timely publication makes a strong case for the relevance of Category V protected areas to the developing world. This could make a real contribution to widening our vision of what is meant by 'protected areas'. And if the advice given here is acted on, it should bring benefits to those planning, managing and indeed living within such important landscape areas around the globe.

Yolanda Kakabadse
Quito, Ecuador, September 2002

1. Introduction

1.1 The background to this publication

We need protected areas for the values and benefits that they bring to society. Such places are broadly of two kinds: those where the emphasis is put on the protection of the natural world (even though this very often requires working with local people), and those where the focus is on maintaining a relationship **between** people and nature. It is this second idea – *that of people and nature together* – which is at the heart of the Protected Landscape approach; or, to use the language of IUCN's protected area categorisation, Category V.

Though there is currently a concentration of Protected Landscapes in Europe, they are to be found in every region of the world: in developed and developing countries, in small island States and continental countries. Many more areas, particularly in the developing world, have the potential to be recognised as Protected Landscapes, because they are rich in natural and cultural values and can be models of sustainability. With the rapid loss or modification of natural (or near-natural) ecosystems, it becomes ever more necessary to protect, or restore, other areas that are important for biodiversity conservation.

In pursuit of sustainable approaches to development, therefore, countries need to look beyond those relatively limited, if vitally important areas in need of strict protection, and include also in their protected area systems lived-in landscapes that are important for economic, social, cultural and environmental reasons. In particular, they should consider using the Category V model as a way to recognise and encourage the sustainable use of natural resources in places that have been shaped by people over long periods of time, and to support human communities that have adopted sustainable practices.

Developing countries especially face many challenges, including those of poverty alleviation, creating better livelihood prospects for their citizens, and helping to protect and enhance local culture and nature against the negative aspects of globalisation. These problems are often particularly acute among vulnerable rural communities. The Category V model can help to empower communities to withstand and overcome such outside pressures. This is especially so in societies where there is a commitment to good governance.

One point needs stressing at the outset: **nothing in these Guidelines is intended to diminish the importance of strictly protected areas**. Indeed, the need for strict protection for areas of high biodiversity, and of the world's remaining threatened natural ecosystems and species, is greater than ever. Rather the requirement is to supplement such protection with other measures that focus on the lived-in landscape.

So IUCN wishes to encourage governments and others to establish and manage Category V protected areas in countries around the world so as to extend the role that protected area systems play in biodiversity conservation and sustainable development. These Guidelines are intended to help do this. In publishing them, IUCN builds on work it has undertaken over the past 15 or more years.

In 1987, IUCN co-hosted a symposium on Protected Landscapes in the Lake District, UK (Countryside Commission 1988). This led directly to an IUCN General Assembly resolution a year later which urged governments and others to give more attention to Category V protected areas. One result was the establishment in 1990 of the International Centre for Protected Landscapes, at Aberystwyth, Wales, UK[1]. In 1992, as a contribution to the IVth World Congress on National Parks and Protected Areas, (Caracas, Venezuela), IUCN published its *Guide on Protected Landscapes for Policy-Makers and Planners*, written by the late P.H.C. (Bing) Lucas (Lucas, 1992). At the same time, the World Heritage Committee agreed to include a Cultural Landscapes category under the World Heritage Convention.

Important developments that have taken place since include:

- The publication of the IUCN *Guidelines for Protected Area Management Categories* (IUCN, 1994), which puts Category V areas – now formally known as Protected Landscapes and Seascapes – on an equal footing with other categories of protected area. The specific advice in the guidelines on Category V is at Annex 1;

- The first IUCN World Conservation Congress, held in Montreal in 1996, adopted a resolution (1.33) on conservation on privately owned land, relating to Category V protected areas;

- In June 1999, IUCN, the QLF/Atlantic Center for the Environment and the Conservation Study Institute co-sponsored an international workshop on the Stewardship of Protected Landscapes, in Vermont, USA (Conservation Study Institute *et al.*, 2001); and

- As a result, the Steering Committee of the IUCN World Commission on Protected Areas (WCPA) set up a Commission Task Force on Category V protected areas, to draw together global expertise and promote the approach[2].

The Task Force, which at that stage included Bing Lucas, soon decided that his 1992 publication needed to be updated. Members of the task force have been primarily responsible for the drafting of these new Guidelines.

1.2 The aim of these guidelines

These Guidelines are in the well-established IUCN/Cardiff University series. They seek to distil and promote best practice in protected area management, and are designed to be of practical value to managers. Other publications in the series are listed in the inside cover, and address such protected area-related topics as financing, indigenous peoples, marine protected areas, effective management and tourism[3].

The specific aim of these present Guidelines is to advise all those with responsibilities for protected areas on the planning and management of Protected Landscapes. So, while the primary audience is a professional one in governments at all levels, among NGOs and elsewhere, the advice should also assist decision-makers,

---

[1] For further information, see www.protected-landscapes.org

[2] For more information about the Task Force, see http://wcpa.iucn.org/theme/landscapes/landscapes.html

[3] All of these are listed in the References at the end of this publication and are available from www.wcpa.iucn.org

politicians and other concerned groups at every level, from local communities to international fora.

This publication is part of a family of outputs developed by the Category V Task Force. Thus while these Guidelines focus on **how** to plan and manage Category V areas, they will be accompanied by a book[4] which will show **why** more Category V protected areas are required. There will also be a special issue of *PARKS* magazine[5] with case studies from around the world, summarising **what** is happening to implement these ideas.

1.3 Structure of guidelines

The remaining sections of these Guidelines are organised as follows:

2: **Background**: *an introduction to Category V protected areas*

3: **Planning**: *guidance on the setting up of a Category V protected area*

4: **Management – principles**: *basic considerations relating to the management of Category V protected areas*

5: **Management – policies**: *advice on the policies to apply in Category V protected areas*

6: **Management – processes and plans**: *advice on how to go about the management of Category V protected areas, including the Management Plan*

7: **Management – means**: *advice on the institutional, financial and staffing aspects of the management of Category V protected areas*

The main body of the text deals with general experience and broad lessons of universal relevance. The key messages for planners and managers are identified in boxes, many of which are highlighted thus as **Guidelines**. 26 brief case studies are also included: many of these are taken from Category V protected areas listed by IUCN, and all aim to bring out relevant experience from real life situations on the ground.

---

[4] "Protected Landscapes: Protected Areas where People Live" by Michael Beresford and Jessica Brown (planned publication date 2003).

[5] *PARKS* **2**: 2003.

2. Background – an introduction to Category V protected areas[1]

2.1 Introducing the concept of landscape

"Landscape" is a difficult word. It has many meanings and is interpreted differently by different people. Some societies have no word for it. However, the European Landscape Convention (ELC), the first international agreement to focus exclusively on the topic, defines it as "an area, as perceived by people, whose character is the result of the action and interaction of natural and/or human factors" (Council of Europe, 2000). In this, and in much of the literature, is the idea that **landscape arises from the interaction of people with their environment over time** (Lennon (ed.), in print; and ICOMOS-UK, 2002).

It follows that landscape is much more than scenery, or even a set of purely physical attributes: the visual aspect of landscape is only the outward face of complex human/nature interactions. Also, landscape often has important associative and spiritual values to communities in many parts of the world. Compared therefore to the thinking behind the establishment and management of many protected areas, where the emphasis is on protecting what is seen as 'natural', the protection of landscape puts people at the heart of the operation – *and indeed requires them to be there.* These relationships can be shown diagrammatically – see Figure 1.

Fig. 1   What landscape is

LANDSCAPE =	*Nature*	PLUS	*People*
LANDSCAPE =	*The past*	PLUS	*The present*
LANDSCAPE =	*Physical attributes (scenery, nature, historic heritage)*	PLUS	*Associative values (social and cultural)*

---

[1] For a fuller consideration of the matters covered in this chapter, see "Protected Landscapes: Protected Areas where People Live" by Michael Beresford and Jessica Brown, to be published in 2003.

5

Landscape as thus conceived is universal, and occurs everywhere. It therefore includes not only terrestrial but also coastal and marine environments – hence the addition of the term 'seascapes' to the IUCN definition, see Section 2.2.4 below.

But while landscape occurs everywhere, it takes many forms and thus gives distinctiveness to place. It is part of everyone's day to day environment: people both shape and are shaped by the immediate landscape around them. Far more than endangered species of wildlife or great cultural monuments, for example, landscape is "an important part of the quality of life for people **everywhere**" and a "key element of individual and social well-being" (from the Preamble of the ELC). It is also often of great local, regional and national economic importance, as the foundation for much of the world's tourism and hence national and local economies.

Furthermore, landscape can be considered both as an environmental resource in its own right, and as a framework for assessing and managing the development process (Benson and Roe, 2000). It is a particularly good medium through which to plan and manage for sustainability because it reflects economic, social, cultural and ecological forces. Landscape may be inherited from the past, but it should be managed for the future.

While landscape is always culturally influenced, it is often rich in biodiversity and other natural values. Many lived-in, working landscapes are important for nature conservation, with valuable habitats and rare species whose continued existence may depend on the survival of traditional forms of land use. Some landscapes reflect specific techniques of sustainable land use, or embody a particular spiritual relationship to nature. Protection of such landscapes, and of the way of life within them so that it can evolve in balance with natural systems, is therefore essential to maintain biological and cultural diversity.

But landscapes can also bear the imprint of past exploitation: for example, in Small Island Developing States of the Caribbean, the pre-colonial landscapes were replaced by those derived from an exploitative system of production using forcibly imported labour. Planning for landscape conservation needs to be sensitive to such history, taking into account that not all heritage conveys positive messages.

The outstanding universal value of some landscapes was recognised by the World Heritage Committee in 1992, when it included Cultural Landscapes as a special type of cultural Word Heritage site. In a sense, all landscape is "cultural", since no part of the earth is immune to human influence of some kind. However, the Committee's decision to include Cultural Landscapes under the convention specifically recognised the international importance of some lived-in, working landscapes – see also Section 3.5.1 (Lennon (ed.), in print).

Because of the intrinsic importance of many landscape areas, and the values attached by society to them, some countries began more than 50 years ago to introduce national legislation etc. to protect those landscapes that they valued most highly. This was initially mostly the case in Europe. Here the approach found favour because of the long history of land settlement, the near absence of large natural areas, the presence of many varied humanised landscapes (many of which were rich in natural values), relatively high population densities and the early development of tourism. Through such legislation, recognition was given to areas which:

   had outstanding scenic qualities;

■ retained strong links between culture and nature;

■ used natural resources sustainably; and

■ maintained their 'integrity', because they had not been disrupted by the impacts of industry, urbanisation or infrastructure (e.g. Green and Vos, 2000, and Council of Europe, 1998).

These areas became the first formally designated Protected Landscapes. But of course people and nature have co-evolved everywhere, and it is now clear that humanised landscapes deserving special recognition are to be found in many parts of the world other than Europe. Furthermore, research has shown that many places that were once thought to be "pristine" natural landscapes were in fact long inhabited and modified by people. Indeed they too are cultural landscapes, and sometimes far more ancient than those in Europe, bearing the imprint of many thousands of years of human activity. For these reasons, the Protected Landscapes approach has now begun to be adopted in countries outside Europe (see, for example, some of the countries listed in Box 3). Moreover, it has the potential to be used much more widely and in many more countries as part of their strategies for national systems of protected areas, biodiversity conservation and sustainable rural development.

2.2 IUCN Protected Area Management Categories

2.2.1 Background to the categories

There are more than 40,000 protected areas in the world (data source: United Nations Environment Programme's World Conservation Monitoring Centre – UNEP-WCMC). They vary greatly in nearly every respect: the precise purposes for which they are managed; the species, ecosystem or landscapes which they protect; their size; the type of management body responsible; the resources available for management; the principal management challenges; the names given to them at the national level – and so forth. To bring some order into this confusing picture, to standardise international terminology, and to promote a range of complementary approaches to protected area planning and management, IUCN has adopted and promoted a categories system for protected areas, based upon the objectives for which they are managed.

2.2.2 The 1978 system of categorisation

The first such system was developed in 1978 (IUCN, 1978). This included a category of protected area which it called 'Protected Landscape'. Rather confusingly, this lumped together two separate ideas: (i) that of areas "whose landscape possess special aesthetic qualities which are the result of the interaction of man (sic) and the land" (ibid. pp. 18); and (ii) those "that are primarily natural areas managed intensively by man for recreational and tourism use" (ibid).

2.2.3 The 1994 system of categorisation

The 1978 system was replaced by the present IUCN protected area management categories system in 1994 (IUCN, 1994). This takes as its starting point the following definition of a protected area, which is intended to apply to *all* categories:

"An area of land and/or sea especially dedicated to the protection and maintenance of biological diversity, and of natural and associated cultural resources, and managed through legal or other effective means." (ibid. page 7).

Key points to note about this definition are:

- it explicitly applies to the marine as well as the terrestrial environment;
- it requires that there should always be a special policy for the conservation of biodiversity (but it need not be the pre-eminent one);
- it allows for conservation of natural resources, and of those cultural resources which are **associated** with these (but not cultural sites **per se**); and
- it requires that a management regime be in place, but acknowledges that in some places this may be done effectively through tradition, customary laws or ownership rather than in a formal legal manner.

Within this broad definition, IUCN has developed a system of six categories of protected areas, as shown in Figure 2.

Fig. 2 The six IUCN Management Categories of Protected Areas (IUCN, 1994)

Category	Description
Ia	*Strict Nature Reserve*: Protected area managed mainly for science.
Ib	*Wilderness Area*: Protected area managed mainly for wilderness protection.
II	*National Park*: Protected area managed mainly for ecosystem protection and recreation.
III	*Natural Monument*: Protected area managed mainly for conservation of specific natural features.
IV	*Habitat/Species Management Area*: Protected area managed mainly for conservation through management intervention.
V	*Protected Landscape/Seascape*: Protected area managed mainly for landscape/ seascape conservation and recreation.
VI	*Managed Resource Protected Area*: Protected area managed mainly for the sustainable use of natural ecosystems.

Key points to note about the system as it is promoted by IUCN are:

- the basis of categorisation is by primary management objective;
- assignment to a category is not a commentary on management effectiveness;
- the categories system is international (and therefore inevitably broad brush);
- national names for protected areas may vary, even though their aims may be the same. Likewise the same name can mean different kinds of protected areas in different countries;
- all categories are important; but
- a gradation of human intervention/ environmental modification is implied.

This last point is illustrated by Figure 3:

Fig. 3   Protected Area Management Categories and degree of environmental modification

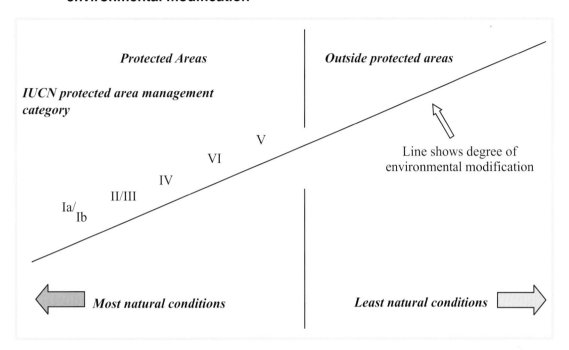

It should be noted in Figure 3 that Category V is, in fact, the protected area category that protects environments where the greatest extent of human modification has taken place.

2.2.4 Category V in the system

The 1994 Guidelines for Protected Area Management Categories defines Category V, Protected Landscape/Seascape thus:

Area of land, with coast and sea as appropriate, where the interaction of people and nature over time has produced an area of distinct character with significant aesthetic, ecological and/or cultural value, and often with high biological diversity. Safeguarding the integrity of this traditional interaction is vital to the protection, maintenance and evolution of such an area.

Note that the term used in the 1978 guidance – Protected Landscape – was replaced in 1994 with 'Protected Landscape/Seascape'. This reflected the view (expressed also in the definition of a protected area – see Section 2.2.1) that protected areas of all kinds were needed for conservation in both terrestrial and marine environments. The inclusion of the less-commonly used term 'seascape' in the category title is meant to signify that some Category V protected areas will be a mix of land and sea – an archipelago, or a combination of islands, peninsulas and inlets, for example[2] (see photo 8). In such areas, the planning approach known as "Coastal Zone Management" will be appropriate (see Clark 1996, and Salm and Clark 2000). The term 'Protected Landscape' is used throughout these guidelines for brevity, but it should be taken as including 'seascape' as appropriate.

---

[2] Several examples of marine protected areas with Category V characteristics are referred to in WCPA's *PARKS* Journal for June 1998, notably the Wadden Sea (Denmark, Germany and the Netherlands) and the Breiðafjöður Conservation Area (Iceland).

Annex 1 contains an extract from the 1994 guidance. It sets out the objectives of management, guidance for selection, and organisational responsibility for Category V areas. These present Guidelines augment and expand on this advice.

As implied by Figure 3, and confirmed by the definition, Category V is unique among the six categories by making the core idea the maintenance of environmental and cultural values where there is a direct **interaction** between people and nature. The focus of management of Category V areas is not on nature conservation *per se*, but about guiding human processes so that the area and its resources are protected, managed and capable of evolving in a sustainable way – and natural and cultural values are thereby maintained and enhanced.

Though this category assumes a large degree of human intervention, it does not follow that it is to be used as a "dumping ground" for protected areas in other categories that have failed in their primary purpose. For example, if the integrity of a Category II National Park is badly affected by development or resource exploitation, this is no reason to assign it to Category V. As noted above the question of management effectiveness is a separate matter from that of management objective. Category V areas need to be managed to just as high a standard as other categories – but for a different purpose.

2.2.5 Category V and Category VI

Though Category V is unique among the categories in its emphasis on **interaction** between people and nature, it shares with Category VI the idea of multiple use, and is often taken together with it as one of the two less strictly protected categories. Also many of the reasons for a growing interest in Category V apply to Category VI as well, for example the emphasis on sustainable use of natural resources. But there is an important difference. Whereas Category V protected areas are lived-in working landscapes that have been extensively modified by people over time, the definition of Category VI speaks of an 'area of predominantly unmodified natural systems', which is to be managed so that at least two thirds of it remain that way. Management in such places is thus generally for long term protection and maintenance of biodiversity, whilst at the same time providing a sustainable flow of goods and services for community needs. Therefore while both categories put people at the heart of the approach, the degree of environmental modification in Category V protected areas will be significantly greater. The differences are summarised in Figure 4.

Fig. 4 Main differences between Categories V and VI

	Category V Protected Area	**Category VI Protected Area**
Core management philosophy	Maintain harmonious interaction of nature and people	Maintain predominantly natural conditions as basis for sustainable livelihoods
Degree of modification of environment (see also Fig. 3)	Considerable: mainly a lived-in, working landscape	Predominantly natural (or near natural) conditions
*Typical **dominant** land uses*	Agriculture, forestry, tourism	Hunting and gathering, grazing, management of natural resources

2.3 Facts and figures

The latest United Nations List of Protected Areas for 1997 (IUCN, 1998) lists all the world's protected areas: a total of 13,321 sites[3]. It also includes some basic information about them, including the management category into which they have been assigned by the country concerned and by UNEP-WCMC. The 1997 UN List contains 3,178 Category V protected area, covering 676,892km^2 in all. Therefore, world wide, Category V areas accounted for 23.8% in terms of the number of all protected areas and 11% in terms of area covered (this information is presented diagrammatically in Figures 5 and 6). It follows that Category V protected areas in the UN list have a relatively small average size.

Fig. 5   The world's protected areas by category and number

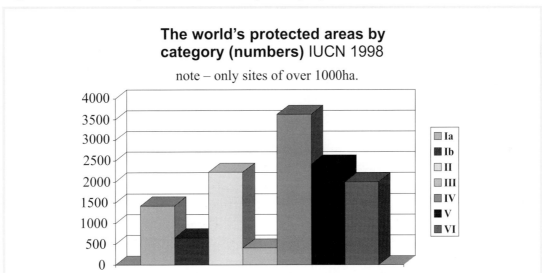

Fig. 6   The world's protected areas by category and extent

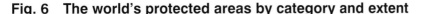

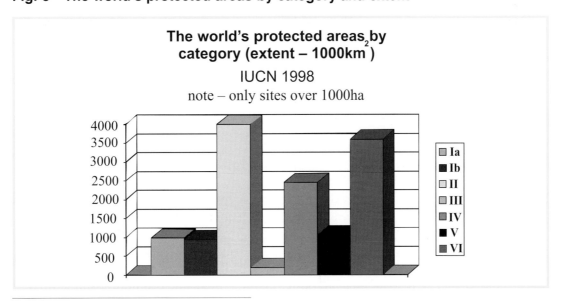

---

[3] The figure is far smaller than the total number of sites on the UNEP-WCMC database, as the UN List omits sites under 1000ha (10km^2), with a lower limit of 100ha for wholly protected offshore or oceanic islands.

In contrast with the global figure, Category V protected areas in Europe account for about two thirds of the protected area estate in this region. The total area thus protected in this region is over a third of a million km^2, or 7.1% of the total land surface, (as against 10.9% for the total proportion of land under protection of all kinds). In a number of European countries – notably Czech Republic, France, Italy, Latvia, Luxembourg, Slovakia, Switzerland and the UK – at least 10% of the entire land area is protected as Category V; in Austria and Germany it is more than 20%.

Also in contrast to the global data, the average size of such areas in Europe tends to be greater than that of other protected area categories. The difference between Europe and elsewhere in this regard may be due to the caution so far shown in using the Protected Landscape categorisation in other parts of the world. IUCN believes this caution is misplaced, and that the principles of Category V protected areas are, in fact, universal and potentially relevant in all regions of the world.

2.4 Key characteristics of Protected Landscapes

With more than 50 years of experience in Europe, and a growing body of experience from elsewhere, it is now possible to identify with confidence the main features which underpin – and drive – the Category V approach. Thus it:

- is concerned with both people **and** their environment;
- is concerned with a range of natural and cultural values;
- focuses on areas where people/nature relationships have produced a landscape with high aesthetic, ecological, biodiversity and/or cultural values, and which retains integrity;
- is both a type of protected area with combinations of special qualities, **and** a management process to guide change;
- reflects a visionary and pro-active approach, aiming to enhance values rather than simply to maintain or protect existing assets;
- views communities, and their traditions, as fundamental to the success of the approach: therefore stakeholder and partnership approaches are required, e.g. co-management (see Box 29);
- recognises the value of, and the need to support, the stewardship role of the private landowner or manager (including that of Land Trusts or similar bodies);
- usually involves management arrangements that are determined by local circumstances and needs, and resolved through decision-making at local government or community levels;
- places a special emphasis on effective land use planning;
- depends therefore on the presence of transparent and democratic structures which support peoples' active involvement in the shaping of their own environment;
- brings social, economic and cultural benefits to local communities;
- brings environmental, cultural, educational and other benefits to a wider public;
- requires that all management activities be integrated, and promote sustainability;
- can be used to help resolve conflicts over resource management;
- can offer models of sustainability for wider application elsewhere in rural areas; and

like all protected areas, requires effective management systems, including setting of objectives, planning, resource allocation, implementation, monitoring, review and feedback.

The core of the Category V approach is built around a set of principles for planning (see Section 3.1) and management (Section 4.1), which may require significant adaptation according to local circumstances, and will evolve over time.

2.5 An approach "whose time has come"

2.5.1 Why an interest in Category V protected areas is timely

Until quite recently, lived-in landscapes had not generally been a focus for much conservation attention at the international level. Several views account for this: that landscape protection in this sense was essentially a Euro-centric idea which had little application elsewhere; that it was superficial concern with how places *look*; and that the global priority was to focus urgently on saving the remaining core "natural" areas. Such views prevailed also because of the dominance of biologists, zoologists and other natural scientists in the conservation movement. Finally there is the power of the essentially North American model of a national park – giving rise to what have been called 'Yellowstone's children' (Everhart, 1972, pp. 200). The result has been a world-wide network of national parks and similar strictly protected areas, which have laid the foundations of much of the present day effort to protect biodiversity.

However, in recent years greater attention has been focused on outstanding, lived-in, working landscapes. This is in large part due to recent, important conceptual and operational advances in conservation in general, and protected areas in particular. Thus, conservation biology has shown the need to work at the ecosystem scale and across the wider landscape, through bio-regional strategies. World-wide, it is now accepted that protected areas can no longer be treated as islands, but must be seen in a larger context. The existence of "paper parks" – protected areas in name only – shows that reliance on regulation and enforcement alone is costly and too often fails. Also, there is a new understanding of the link between nature and culture: healthy landscapes are shaped by human culture as well as the forces of nature; rich biological diversity often coincides with cultural diversity; and conservation cannot be undertaken without the involvement of those people closest to the resources (Brown and Mitchell 2000).

All these trends set the scene for a new inclusive approach to protected areas. This has been captured in a new "paradigm for protected areas", see Figure 7.

In several ways, the emergence of such new thinking about protected areas as a whole increases the significance of Category V protected areas (and to some extent Category VI), since they demonstrate many of the characteristics of the right hand column of Figure 7.

In addition, Category V protected areas (and again Category VI to some degree) are also receiving more attention because they:

- are seen as a means of identifying, supporting and promoting sustainable resource use, which is especially valuable where there are storehouses of traditions and tried and well-tested practices that can be drawn upon in using natural resources sustainably (e.g. Benson and Roe, 2000);

13

Fig. 7 A new paradigm for protected areas (after Beresford and Phillips, 2000)

As it was: protected areas were ...	As it is becoming: protected areas are ...
Planned and managed against people	Run with, for, and in some cases by local people
Run by central government	Run by many partners
Set aside for conservation	Run also with social and economic objectives
Managed without regard to local community	Managed to help meet needs of local people
Developed separately	Planned as part of national, regional and international systems
Managed as 'islands'	Developed as 'networks' (strictly protected areas, buffered and linked by green corridors)
Established mainly for scenic protection	Often set up for scientific, economic and cultural reasons
Managed mainly for visitors and tourists	Managed with local people more in mind
Managed reactively within short timescale	Managed adaptively with long-term perspective
About protection	Also about restoration and rehabilitation
Viewed primarily as a national asset	Viewed also as a community asset
Viewed exclusively as a national concern	Viewed also as an international concern

- are key elements in large-scale conservation programmes known as bio-regional planning, ecosystem management, ecosystem-based management or landscape scale planning (e.g. Miller, 1996; Maltby *et al.*, 1999);

- can buttress, buffer or support more strictly protected areas, such as Categories I–IV;

- can perform a similar role as "building blocks" in biological or ecological corridors (e.g. Bennett, 1998);

- offer scope for the restoration of natural and cultural values as well as for their protection;

- are regarded as a meeting ground between the cultural and natural heritage, notably through the inclusion of Cultural Landscapes under the World Heritage Convention;

- are a very flexible way of managing an area, capable of taking many different forms according to the local situation (see Box 32 for example);

- often include agricultural systems and other land use practices that depend on, and conserve, a rich genetic heritage of domesticated livestock and crops, whose potential value is increasingly appreciated (e.g. through the work programme of the Convention on Biological Diversity – CBD); and

- reflect the public's wish at any rate, to have access to a high-quality landscape. (Within Europe, this right is now formally incorporated in the preamble to the ELC, see Box 7).

2.5.2 Using Category V approaches outside Europe and in the developing world

It is against such a background that there is now a growing interest in Category V approaches to conservation in many countries. Most significantly, the interest is no longer confined to Europe. Thus there has been on-the-ground action to set up Category V protected areas, and calls for similar measures, in many other regions, for example in:

- the Small Island Developing States in the Caribbean and the Pacific (Romulus and Lucas, 2000);
- the traditional farming lands of the Andes (Sarmiento *et al*, 2000);
- the traditional coffee growing areas of Mexico and Central America (Miller *et al.*, 2001);
- the long settled landscapes of eastern parts of the USA and Canada (Mitchell *et al.,* 2002) – see photos 5 and 7;
- the growth, in the US national park system, of new protected areas relying on partnerships (Tuxill and Mitchell, (eds.), 2001);
- wildlife dispersal areas of East Africa;
- the ancient 'himas' reserve and irrigation systems of Saudi Arabia (Joubert and Sulayem, 1994);
- the mountain communities of the Himalayas, e.g. the Annapurna Conservation Area, Nepal – see photos 4 and 11;
- Japan, where many national parks are managed as Category V protected areas (WCMC, 1987);
- the rice terraces of the Philippines (Conklin, 1980).

A number of these examples are further described in case study boxes throughout this publication and/or illustrated in the photographs. As will be apparent, many are taken from the developing world. Box 1 summarises why developing countries should take an interest in the approach:

Box 1. Why Category V approaches are well-suited to developing countries' needs

With its emphasis on the value of the interactions between people and nature over time, the Category V (Protected Landscape and Seascape) designation can be particularly appropriate for lived-in landscapes in developing regions of the world. In particular, it is a useful approach because it:

- links people's needs and livelihoods to the conservation and sustainable use of natural resources and hence biodiversity;
- typically comprises a mosaic of land ownership patterns, including private and communally owned property;
- can accommodate, and increase respect for diverse management regimes, including customary laws and religious observance governing resource management;
- has important specific objectives related to conservation of cultural heritage;
- seeks to bring benefits to local communities and contribute to their well-being, through the provision of environmental goods and services; and
- has proven to work well in certain places where strict protected areas have failed because of the difficulties of securing support from local communities.

(After Oviedo and Brown, 1999)

It is not suggested that a type of protected area that had strong roots in Europe should now just be transposed to the developing world in its original form: that would be to run the risk of repeating mistakes made with other inappropriate park models in the past. Rather it is argued that some inherent characteristics of the Category V approach make it suitable for consideration in many more countries, including developing ones. As the case studies in these Guidelines make clear, these characteristics include:

- the fact that the management of Category V protected areas can take many different forms, and can therefore be adapted to a variety of local needs and situations;

- the recognition it gives to traditional land management systems which deserve to be protected for their sustainable values;

- the protection it can give to natural resources, biodiversity and landscape values that occur in many lived-in rural areas of developing countries, but are not normally included in protected area systems;

- the fact that it represents an alternative to strictly protected areas, which in some places have been resisted by local communities and have had rather limited conservation achievements; and

- the way that it offers new models for conservation and sustainable development that involve partnerships with local communities and other stakeholders.

Of course Category V protected areas cannot hope to solve all the development and conservation challenges facing developing countries. Nor are they a convenient means of avoiding all painful trade-offs between development and conservation, as the conservation of such places will always involve constraints over some kinds of development. Also, as already noted, Category V protected areas are no substitute for more conventional forms of protected areas (i.e. those of Categories I–IV), whose importance is greater than ever. Rather the need now is to complement strict protection with the wider adoption of the Category V approach. These Guidelines aim to show how protected areas of this kind should be planned and managed.

3. The planning of Category V protected areas

3.1 Principles of Category V planning

In setting out principles (both here and in Section 4.1), it is recognised that it may be difficult for some countries, and some protected area planners and managers, to adopt them in full at this stage. They represent, therefore, statements of what is desirable, and towards which those responsible for the planning and management of Category V areas should aspire.

The term "planning" is used here to mean the process that leads up to the establishment of a protected area (after which "management" becomes the operative word). This section therefore deals with the legal framework, and the processes of selection and establishment. It has several dimensions:

- A local dimension, in which the necessary measures are put in place before each area is formally established. At this stage, questions will arise about the legal status for the area, the objectives set for it, and the management structures, boundaries etc. that are decided upon;

- Where a regional (i.e. sub-national) level of governance has been developed, a regional dimension, in which the individual protected area(s) are planned as part of regional land use and economic development;

- A national dimension, involving the planning of a *system* of Category V protected areas. This encompasses such issues as the essential legislative foundation, national data collection, clarification of broad aims for Category V protected areas and the incorporation of Protected Landscapes within a national system of protected areas and policies relating to change within rural areas; and

- An international dimension, since countries have certain international environmental or heritage obligations which have implications for the planning of protected areas in general, and in some cases for Protected Landscapes. Some of these arise from global conventions like the CBD, Ramsar (Wetlands) and World Heritage, and the UNESCO Man and Biosphere Programme (Biosphere Reserves); and some are regional obligations, such as those under the European Landscape Convention and the Central American Council for Sustainable Development. Also the planning of some Category V protected areas may be affected by bilateral co-operative agreements between neighbouring States relating to environmental and natural resource issues.

Much of these Guidelines have been written from the standpoint of a central, provincial or local government, which aims to set up Category V protected areas. But the initiative to create such areas may also come from others: an NGO, a private entity or the community itself (see also Box 32). **References to the 'protected area agency' or 'protected area authority' should therefore be read with this broad interpretation**

in mind. While circumstances will vary from country to country, it will usually be the case that a supportive legal and administrative framework will be needed if initiatives to set up and manage Category V protected areas that come from outside government are to be successful. And they will not flourish unless good governance is the norm, and the society concerned is committed to the alleviation of poverty, promoting greater equity and encouraging productive livelihoods for all.

The principles for the planning of Category V protected areas are as follows:

Principle 1: *Planning at all levels should be based on the laws, customs and values of the society concerned.* This means, for example, that the general guidance given in this publication should be adapted to the conditions of the country and local society.

Principle 2: *A strong legal basis is required for Category V protected areas* (Section 3.2).

Principle 3: *A systematic approach is needed to the selection of Category V protected areas* (3.3).

Principle 4: *A Category V protected area should be planned with a view to links with other protected areas and the broader bio-region of which it is a part, and as a model of sustainability for potentially wider application* (3.4).

Principle 5: *Consideration should be given to the relevance of any international classification of protection* (3.5).

Principle 6: *The determination of the protected area boundaries is a key part of planning* (3.6).

Principle 7: *Planning systems should be flexible enough to accommodate existing land ownership patterns and institutional roles where these can support the aims of conservation* (5.2.2).

Principle 8: *An effective system of land use planning is an essential foundation* (5.4).

Principle 9: *Planning must involve participation by a range of national, regional and local interests* (3.7).

Principle 10: *Building a strong political and public constituency in support of the area is essential* (3.8).

3.2 Legislation for Category V protected areas

It is conventional to think of legislation as the necessary foundation for a Category V protected area, but – as suggested above – there are many places worthy of protection which have not yet been given formal, legal recognition. While this does not diminish the importance of a strong legal base, it is a reminder that successful Category V protected areas depend upon social acceptance and tradition as well.

An effective legal basis is normally essential, however, in order to set up and manage a Category V protected area. This may be of one of three kinds: (i) protected areas legislation; (ii) land use controls and other legislation directed at elements of the landscape (de Klemm in IUCN, 2000); and (iii) general legislation favouring sustainable development.

Protected Area Legislation: an increasing number of countries have specifically included landscape protection as part of their protected area legislation, especially where they have set out to follow the IUCN protected area management categories system (see Figure 2). In general, these form part of the nature conservation laws of the country, although separate laws on landscape protection can also be found. Where a law specifically authorises the creation of landscape protected areas (i.e. where it includes protection of landscapes and seascapes as one of the justifications for designating a protected area), there are many different approaches to the nature of, and procedures involved in such designation.

A few countries may establish individual Category V areas by provision in their statutes. However, more often those statutes serve a general enabling function, under which the responsibility for establishing individual Category V protected areas is assigned to a particular agency or other governmental unit (the legislation of some countries allows for other groups, such as NGOs, to play the role of 'agency'). This will establish the protection by adopting subordinate legislation, making an administrative declaration or following other designated procedures. An important role of such legislation is to express the relative priorities of environmental, economic and social objectives. Though these guidelines stress the need for integration between all three purposes, there is value in a strong statement that makes clear that – when there is an unavoidable conflict – environmental protection should have the prior claim (see Case Study 2).

Land use legislation: more commonly, landscape-related issues – see also Box 1 – are addressed in land use planning legislation. Here again, varied approaches are possible. Some countries utilise their land use legislative framework as the primary vehicle for formally designating landscape protected areas – in essence, it operates as a protected areas law. In other cases, landscape protected areas, although not specifically designated as such, are created *de facto* by laws which limit activities within the landscape zone in a manner identical to a protected area. The role of land use planning is particularly critical to the success of Protected Landscapes but is dealt with very differently in different countries.

General provisions on sustainable development: finally, a few countries have incorporated the notion of sustainable development, and Agenda 21, into legislative form (e.g. in the wording of the constitution). While such expressions of intent are still very general, they may assist the case for Category V protected areas.

Given the wide range of situations between countries, and the variety of legal traditions, it is not appropriate to prescribe a single approach to the legal foundations for all Category V protected areas. But some guidance can be recommended – see Box 2 below.

Box 2. *Guidelines* for legislation for establishment of Category V protected areas

The legislation specifically designed for Category V protected areas should:

- enable the creation of Category V protected areas (either directly through the legislation itself or through a formal process derived from it);
- set down the objectives for such areas in general terms, including recognition that, in these areas, the relationship between environmental, social and economic objectives must be evaluated and managed, but giving priority to the protection of the environmental qualities of the area;
- specify requirements for public and community involvement in the decision-making process for planning and management, including the designation of the area, and giving priority to local residents, but not forgetting that communities, individuals, organisations and entities from outside the area may also be affected and must be given appropriate opportunity;
- define appropriate boundaries for the protected area, or clarify the procedures for their definition, for determining those boundaries with precision, and for addressing the concerns of landowners whose property is within the area designated; also for boundary adjustment;
- enable the establishment and oversight of a competent managing authority;
- set down the powers (e.g. over land use) and duties (e.g. to prepare a management plan) of the authority; and
- explain how the authority will be resourced, staffed etc.

Legislation in other sectors should have due regard to the needs of Category V protected areas. This is especially relevant to legislation in the following areas:

- land use planning and urban development;
- nature, historic and cultural conservation;
- pollution controls;
- the use of water resources, including fisheries;
- agriculture, forestry, fisheries, mining/gravel extraction;
- any geographically-focused legislation, such as that relating to the coastline or wetlands, which will help in managing the area; and
- activities of other statutory bodies, utilities and public service providers, including especially infrastructure development and rural livelihood improvement programmes.

Case Studies 1 and 2 are examples of national legislation used to set up national systems of Category V areas.

CASE STUDY 1.
Brazilian legislation for Environmental Protection Areas (Category V)

Inspired by French and Portuguese experience, and aware of the high cost of land expropriation to create strictly protected areas, Brazil developed an alternative solution to protected area establishment. Thus legislation to establish Environmental Protection Areas (Area de Proteçao Ambiental – APA) was passed in 1981. This focused on areas with a degree of human occupation, but also with special biotic, non-biotic, aesthetic or cultural values which are important for the quality of life and well-being of human populations. Many legal tools have been used to establish rules and guidelines for such areas. However, the most important was a federal law of 2000, which gave them proper status as Conservation Units within the National System of Conservation Units (SNUC). By 1997, 86 such areas had been set up in Brazil, in 21 states (covering nearly 11.6 million km^2 – or about 22% of all Brazil's protected areas). The SNUC has 12 classes of protected areas, in two broad groups: integral protection (five classes) and sustainable use (seven classes, including the APA).

According to the legislation, an APA must have:

- ecological and economic zoning;
- a wildlife zone (Zona de Vida Silvestre – ZVS);
- urban requirements, where appropriate;
- a Management Committee to undertake co-ordination, according to
- a Management Plan.

Source: Marilia Britto de Moraes

CASE STUDY 2.
UK national parks legislation – designed as a partnership

Despite their name, national parks in the UK are protected landscapes, containing much of the nation's finest coast and countryside. Arrangements for their selection, designation and management were embodied in the *National Parks and Access to the Countryside Act 1949*, which applied to England and Wales. The thinking behind the 1949 Act remains broadly valid today, though changing circumstances have led to some revisions. 11 National Parks exist in England and Wales, two more are proposed. Over 250,000 people live in the parks, which cover over 9% of England and Wales. Scotland's National Park legislation was not enacted till 2000 and its first park was established in 2002.

The legislation gives Government Agencies (the Countryside Agency in England, the Countryside Council of Wales and Scottish Natural Heritage) powers to designate national parks and advise on their administration and management. An autonomous National Park Authority (NPA) runs each park. Though they operate within the local government framework, they receive most of their funds from central government. They are corporate bodies with executive powers, whose members are appointed to reflect local and national interests.

Cont.

CASE STUDY 2.
UK national parks legislation – designed as a partnership (cont.)

In England and Wales, NPAs have a range of powers to accomplish their twin purposes:

- to conserve and enhance the natural beauty, wildlife and cultural heritage; and

- to promote public understanding and enjoyment of the park's special qualities.

If conflict between these purposes cannot be resolved, priority must go to the first. However, whilst national parks are not economic development agencies, NPAs are required to fulfil their twin purposes in a way that fosters the social and economic well-being of their local communities. NPAs produce a land use and a Management Plan for the area, provide management services, and control building and other kinds of development.

Source: Richard Partington

One question, which is bound to arise at this stage, is the name to be given to Category V areas under national legislation. The generic title used by IUCN is "Protected Landscapes/Seascapes", but, as noted above, the names given at the national level to protected areas in each category will vary, in response to national or even local circumstances and needs. Box 3 below gives an indication of the range of names that have been used in a number of countries (in translation where necessary) to describe their Category V protected areas.

Box 3. Some examples of national names used for Category V Protected Areas (IUCN, 1998)

Austria: Protected Landscape

Brazil: Environmental Protection Areas

Canada (Ontario): Conservation Area

Canada (Québec): Nature Park

China: Scenic Area

China (Hong Kong): Country Park

Colombia: Protection Forest Reserve

Croatia: Protected Landscape and Nature Park

Cuba: Touristic Natural Area

Czech Republic: Protected Landscape Area

Dominican Republic: Protected Landscape

France: Regional Nature Park

Germany: Landscape Protection Area/Nature Park

Hungary: Landscape Protected Area

Italy: Regional or Provincial Nature Park

Japan: National Park (some)

Korea, Republic of: National Park

Latvia: Protected Landscape and Nature Park

New Zealand: Conservation Park

Norway: Landscape Protection Area

Philippines: Protected Landscape/Seascape

Poland: Landscape Park

Portugal: Nature Park and Protected Landscape

Saudi Arabia: Hima Traditional Reserve

Slovenia: Landscape Park

Spain: Nature Park

Sweden: Nature Conservation Area

Switzerland: Landscape Protection Area

Turkey: Nature Park

UK: National Park, Area of Outstanding Natural Beauty and National Scenic Area

Cont.

> **Box 3. Some examples of national names used for Category V Protected Areas (IUCN, 1998) (cont.)**
>
> USA: many different terms are used at State level
>
> Venezuela: Protective Zone
>
> Yugoslavia: Regional Nature Park
>
> Zimbabwe: Recreation Park
>
> *Notes on Box 3:*
>
> 1. Information from the United Nations List of Protected Areas, 1997 (IUCN, 1998).
> 2. This is not a complete list of all Category V protected areas in the UN list, only a selection.
> 3. No judgement is implied about how far the above sites meet the standards advocated in these guidelines.

3.3 Selection of Category V protected areas

Usually legislation will be enabling, and the act of selecting individual areas that are suitable for Category V status should follow. The IUCN 1994 guidelines on the protected area management categories (see Annex 1) give only limited advice on the criteria to be used at this stage. However, it is possible to identify some essential and desirable qualities that should be looked for at the selection stage, see Box 4.

> **Box 4. *Guidelines* on the criteria for selecting Category V Protected Areas**
>
> ***Essential*** *characteristics in the selection of Category V protected areas, which should be of national or international significance:*
>
> - Landscape and/or coastal and island seascape of high and/or distinct scenic quality;
> - Significant associated habitats, and flora and fauna;
> - Evidence that a harmonious interaction between people and nature has endured over time, and still has integrity;
> - Unique or traditional land-use patterns, e.g. as evidenced in human settlements;
> - Valued for the provision of environmental services (e.g. watershed protection);
> - Valued for the sustainable use of natural resources;
> - Unique or traditional social organisations, as evidenced in local customs, livelihoods and beliefs; and
> - Opportunities for public enjoyment through recreation and tourism consistent with life style and economic activities.
>
> ***Desirable*** *characteristics in the selection of Category V protected areas:*
>
> - Suitability for scientific research;
> - Important for education;
> - Recognition by artists of all kinds and in cultural traditions (now and in the past);
> - Important for agri-biodiversity (domesticated livestock and crops); and
> - Potential for ecological and /or landscape restoration.

Selection should be systematic, not *ad hoc*. In other words, the best approach is a thorough, country-wide analysis of areas that are most suitable for Category V status rather that individual, random site selection exercises. Ideally such country-wide analyses should form part of the response to the requirements of Article 8a of the CBD, which requires each State Party to establish "a system of protected areas, or areas where special measures need to be taken, to conserve biological diversity". The analyses of sites for World Heritage Cultural Landscapes (see below) may also help to identify suitable sites for Category V protected areas.

IUCN has published general advice on the development of national system plans for protected areas – systems, that is, that include Category V areas (Davey, 1998). However, the specific features of Category V protected areas require a particular emphasis upon some aspects of the lived-in, working landscape that will not usually be covered by a normal biodiversity assessment, since these tend to focus on the remaining natural or near-natural habitats. Some countries, notably in Europe, have undertaken landscape analyses to help them develop landscape-related policies, including the identification of areas suitable for Category V protected areas (Wascher, 2000). This is a promising area, but it is too early to recommend a standard approach, given the wide range of differing circumstances between different countries. However it is clear that the selection of Category V protected areas will require data from a variety of sources, see Box 5.

Box 5. *Guidelines* on the information required to select Category V protected areas

*Note that this advice **supplements** general principles for selection of sites for a national system of protected areas (see Davey, 1998)*

In selecting sites at the national level for designation as possible Category V protected areas, information will be needed on the following:

Scenic quality: areas with exceptional or dramatic scenery, deriving as much from the contrast and/or interaction between the works of nature and humanity as from the intrinsic quality of the natural features themselves;

Recreational importance: areas where the landscape and the cultural associations are both important attractions for tourists or for outdoor leisure activities;

Traditions of stewardship: areas where the people have long and living traditions of care for the land and its natural resources, based upon the principles of sustainability, and in particular those that reflect excellent examples of sustainable land use by:

- respecting the productive capability of land,
- conserving the quality and quantity of soil,
- managing and safeguarding water quality,
- managing the marine environment responsibly,
- managing streams and rivers so as to reduce damaging floods and run-off,
- maintaining plant cover, and
- restoring vegetation, soils and sources of water;

Biodiversity conservation: areas where the landscape represents an outstanding example of how traditional land use patterns can:

- contribute to the protection of natural ecosystems (e.g. by providing for the protection of watershed forests),
- help protect wild species of fauna or flora,

Cont.

> **Box 5. *Guidelines* on the information required to select Category V protected areas (cont.)**
>
> help protect genetic diversity within wild species, and
>
> create semi-natural habitats of great importance to biodiversity, i.e. manipulated eco-systems with well-structured and functional interactions between its living components;
>
> **Agri-biodiversity**: Areas where traditional farm systems have:
>
> developed and/or conserved a wide range of varieties of domesticated livestock, and
>
> developed and/or conserved a wide range of varieties of cultivated crops, such as cereals, fruit or root vegetables;
>
> **Cultural heritage**: landscapes that retain built features from the past, testifying to the occurrence of important events and/or a history of human occupation over many years; and
>
> **Cultural associations**: areas whose landscape embodies strong cultural values, and/or artistic associations.

Thus the assessment of sites for possible inclusion in a national system plan as Category V protected areas requires consideration of some environmental, cultural, economic and social factors, and of the interaction between them, that are not normally considered in planning protected area systems. It also requires that both tangible and intangible resources and benefits are taken into account.

3.4 Category V, neighbouring protected areas and bio-regional planning

A range of geographical relationships between Category V and other protected areas is possible (see also Figure 8), as follows:

In some cases, an extensive Category V protected area may include one or more small reserves for strict protection. Many protected areas in Europe exhibit this feature;

An important function of some Category V protected areas is to act as a buffer around a larger core of a more strictly protected area. As a buffer, a Protected Landscape can help ensure that land use activities do not threaten the integrity of the core protected area, which is normally defined as Categories I–IV (an example of a Category V protected area functioning in this way is described in Case Study 3 from Nepal);

In other cases, a Category V protected area can act as a link between several other protected areas, supporting the ecological benefits of connectivity; and finally

The most ambitious role for Protected Landscapes is to be "building blocks" within a large-scale, sub-regional scheme for conservation, helping to create a corridor for wildlife and deliver the benefits of greater connectivity over maybe several hundred kilometres (Bennett, 1999). Among examples of this kind of bio-regional planning which include Category V areas are:

the Meso-American Biological Corridor, which aims to link together many protected areas of various kinds along the spine of Meso-America;

Fig. 8   Diagrammatic representation of the buffer and linkage functions of a Category V protected area

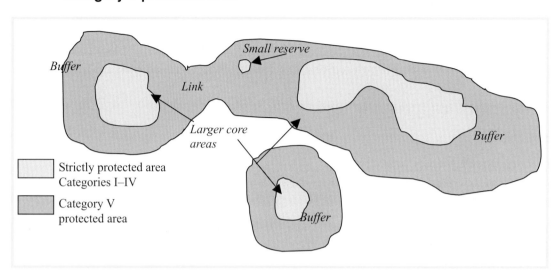

the Serra do Mar, Brazil, which aims to do likewise along the bio-diverse rich south east uplands of that country; and

the Central Appennines Conservation Corridor, Italy, which creates a chain of protection along the Appennine Hills, linked to the core area of Abruzzo National Park.

A Category V protected area which forms part of such a large-scale scheme should still meet the criteria in Box 4. However, the area is clearly of greater strategic value to conservation and sustainable land use when it is part of a region-wide approach to the protection of biodiversity, and of a mosaic of protected areas and other land uses.

CASE STUDY 3
The Royal Chitwan National Park, Nepal – A Category V Buffer Zone

A Buffer Zone (BZ) Regulation was enacted in 1994, allowing park authorities to designate adjoining areas as BZs, and allocate between 30–50% of park revenue for their management. This was done to provide alternative natural resource-based livelihood opportunities to BZ communities, and so reduce their dependence on park resources.

The Royal Chitwan National Park (RCNP) BZ was declared in 1996, with an area of 766km^2 and a population of over 200,000 living in about 510 settlements. About 43% of the BZ is still forested. Some of these forest patches are important as animal refuges and corridors linking RCNP with mountain ecosystems to the north and Indian Wildlife Sanctuaries to the south. RCNP and its BZ also contain important cultural and historical sites. The BZ area is inhabited by various indigenous and hill migrant ethnic groups with impressive cultural and religious values and customs.

A co-management approach has been adopted in the BZ. A BZ Development Council (BZDC) links local people and park management, and mobilises a share of park revenue for conservation and development activities in the BZ, managed through users' committees and groups. User Committees submit their bids to BZDC

Cont.

CASE STUDY 3
The Royal Chitwan National Park, Nepal – A Category V Buffer Zone (cont.)

after consultation and endorsement from users' meetings. To date, approximately US$700,000 park income has gone to BZ management in this way. Various projects, including UNDP-funded Park and People Project, support this initiative.

Though the BZ is not officially designated as a Category V protected area, its character and management aims are similar.

Source: Prabhu Budhathoki

3.5 Category V protected areas and international conventions and classifications

Designation of a Category V protected area is normally a role for central or provincial government, within national legislation. However some such areas may also gain recognition under an international convention or programme. UNESCO's World Heritage Convention and Biosphere Reserve programme are particularly relevant at the global level.

3.5.1 The World Heritage Convention

Since 1992, the World Heritage Committee has been able to include "Cultural Landscapes" in the World Heritage list. Box 6 summarises the advice given by the Committee on this type of World Heritage site. As will be apparent, some such areas are likely to be Category V protected areas at the national level.

Box 6. Cultural Landscapes under the World Heritage Convention

The following is an extract on Cultural Landscapes from the Operational Guidelines[1] to the World Heritage Convention, which govern the implementation of the convention (UNESCO, 1999):

Cultural landscapes "are illustrative of the evolution of human society and settlement over time, under the influence of physical constraints and/or opportunities presented by their natural environment and of successive social, economic and cultural forces, both external and internal. They should be selected on the basis both of their outstanding universal value and of their representativity in terms of a clearly defined geo-cultural region and also for their capacity to illustrate the essential and distinct cultural elements of such regions" (para. 36).

"The term 'cultural landscape' embraces a diversity of manifestations of the interaction between humankind and its natural environment"(para. 37).

"Cultural landscapes often reflect specific techniques of sustainable land use, considering the characteristics and limits of the natural environment they are established in, and a specific spiritual relation to nature. Protection of cultural landscapes

Cont.

---

[1] The World Heritage Operational Guidelines were under review at the time of writing. This section is expected to be included, unamended, in the revised guidelines.

Box 6. Cultural Landscapes under the World Heritage Convention (cont.)

can contribute to modern techniques of sustainable land use and can maintain or enhance natural values in the landscape. The continued existence of traditional forms of land use supports biological diversity in many regions of the world. The protection of traditional cultural landscapes is therefore helpful in maintaining biological diversity" (para. 38).

Three kinds of Cultural Landscape are recognised:

(i) **Landscapes designed and created intentionally by people**: examples are gardens and parklands constructed for aesthetic reasons.

(ii) **Organically evolved landscapes**: these result from an interaction between a social, economic, administrative and/or religious imperative and the natural environment. Two forms exist:

> A relict or fossil landscape where the evolutionary process has ceased;

> A continuing landscape where the evolutionary processes continue to this day, with an active social role in contemporary society closely linked with the traditional way of life, at the same time exhibiting significant material evidence of its evolution over time.

(iii) **Associative cultural landscapes**: these are landscapes which are important by virtue of the powerful religious, artistic or cultural associations of the natural elements, rather than material cultural evidence.

It is apparent that some of the ideas behind the development of World Heritage Cultural Landscapes are similar to those of Category V. This is especially so in: (a) the emphasis placed on human/nature interaction, most notably in the continuing form of organically evolved cultural landscape (type (ii)), which acknowledges the value of landscape-related cultural traditions that continue to this day; and (b) in the importance placed upon associative values (type (iii)) (von Droste *et al.*, 1995).

However, there are also important differences. In Protected Landscapes, "the natural environment, biodiversity conservation and ecosystem integrity have been the primary emphases. In contrast, the emphasis in Cultural Landscapes has been on human history, continuity of cultural traditions, and social values and aspirations". (Mitchell and Buggey, 2000, pp. 35). Moreover, World Heritage Cultural Landscapes include a designed type of landscape (type (i)) that is not reflected in the IUCN notion of a Category V protected area (though a Protected Landscape may include important designed features). Finally, the fundamental criterion for recognition of a World Heritage Cultural Landscape is that of "outstanding universal value". There is less stress placed on outstanding qualities in the case of Category V protected areas, although the areas should certainly be nationally significant to merit protection[2]. See also Figure 10 below.

Linking 'culture' and 'nature' through Cultural Landscapes under the convention represented an important advance. Since its adoption, there has been co-operation in the

---

[2] For a fuller discussion of the relationship of Cultural Landscapes under the World Heritage Convention and Protected Landscapes/IUCN Category V, see Mitchell and Buggey, 2000.

co-ordinated or joint evaluation and monitoring of such sites by IUCN and ICOMOS (natural and cultural advisers respectively to the convention). Based on experience to date, guidelines on the management of Cultural Landscapes are under development for UNESCO (Lennon (ed), in print). These have been drawn on at various places in drafting these present Guidelines on the related topic of Protected Landscapes.

Case study 4 describes how international recognition as a World Heritage Cultural Landscape has been used to focus on the need for urgent action to protect the Philippines Cordilleras rice terraces.

CASE STUDY 4.
The Philippine Rice Terraces – the importance of World Heritage designation (see cover photo and photo 12)

The Rice Terraces of the Philippine Cordilleras (in northern Luzon) were placed on the World Heritage list in 1995. They are among the most inspiring human-shaped landscapes in the world, being of great beauty and drama. Many of them are built on very steep slopes, some exceeding 45°. They are the work of the Ifugao people, and are believed to be over 2000 years old. They are an excellent example of the interweaving of natural and cultural values in a sustainable manner. The site was the first World Heritage cultural landscape in the organically evolving category (see Box 6). Though not formally designated as a Category V protected area, the terrace landscape clearly meets the criteria.

World Heritage designation has focused international attention on the terraces and on their vulnerability to economic and social forces that are leading to physical erosion and decay. Following reports that negative influences continued after designation, an IUCN/ICOMOS mission took place in 2001, after which the World Heritage Committee placed the site on the World Heritage in Danger list. This signalled international concern about the fate of the area. Early in 2002, the Philippine Government disbanded the Task Force previously responsible for co-ordinated management of the site, and initiated action to set up a new body for this purpose. The Committee also voted a sum of money to support national action to implement the recommendations of the IUCN/ICOMOS mission. The long-term prospects for the terraces remain uncertain, but international action under the convention appears the best way to counter the destructive trends that would otherwise continue unabated.

Source: Adrian Phillips

3.5.2 UNESCO Biosphere Reserves

The buffer zone and linking functions of Category V protected areas (see Section 3.4 above) can be very relevant in the context of a Biosphere Reserve. Guidance published by IUCN and UNESCO (Bridgewater *et al.*, 1996) makes clear that Category V protected areas can fulfil the functions of a Buffer or Transition Zone within a Biosphere Reserve, see Figure 9.

Fig. 9   Relationship between IUCN Protected Area Management Categories and Biosphere Reserve Zones (from Bridgewater *et al.,* 1996)

IUCN Protected Area Management Category	Biosphere Reserve Zones		
	Core	Buffer	Transition
I to IV	yes	no	no
V	no	yes	perhaps
VI	perhaps	yes	perhaps

Note: yes = compatibility of management purposes; no = incompatibility of management purposes; perhaps = management purpose may be compatible

3.5.3   Other international agreements

Nationally designated Protected Landscapes, or at least parts of them, may also be recognised under other global agreements (e.g. the Ramsar (wetlands) Convention), and regional agreements (e.g. Natura 2000 in Europe).

As noted above, the European Landscape Convention (ELC), which was opened for signature in 2000, is at present the only international agreement that exclusively addresses landscape issues. It has implications for all the countries covered by the Council of Europe (all the States of geographical Europe, including Russia and several other countries of the former Soviet Union) – see Box 7.

Box 7.   The European Landscape Convention (ELC)[3]

The ELC will come into force when 10 Member States have ratified it. Its aim is "to promote landscape protection, management and planning, and to organise European co-operation on landscape issues" (Article 3). The ELC is concerned with all landscapes, including "natural, rural, urban and peri-urban areas" (Article 2), and does not therefore concentrate on areas that would merit recognition as Protected Landscapes. Nonetheless it is important for Category V protected areas because it raises the importance of landscape issues in general, and specifically requires all signatories to:

recognise landscape in national law;

Cont.

---

[3] For full text of the ELC in English and French, see the web site of the Council of Europe http://conventions.coe.int/treaty/EN/cadreprincipal.htm

> **Box 7. The European Landscape Convention (ELC) (cont.)**
>
>   ▪ develop policies for landscape protection, management and planning;
>
>   ▪ develop procedures for public participation in landscape matters;
>
>   ▪ integrate landscape into regional and town planning policies and others which can impact on the landscape;
>
>   ▪ adopt specific policies on matters such as awareness-raising, training and education, identification and assessment of landscapes, the development of landscape quality objectives and the introduction of policies for landscape protection, management and planning; and
>
>   ▪ co-operate at the European level in relation to policies and programmes, mutual assistance and exchange of information, transfrontier landscapes (see below), a Landscape Award for the Council of Europe, and monitoring of the implementation of the Convention.

Though the ELC is geographically limited in its impact, it may offer a model for future regional co-operation on landscape issues elsewhere in the world. Moreover, individual non-European countries could consider the relevance to their own circumstances of a number of the general principles that it promotes.

Figure 10 sets out in tabular form the main characteristics that distinguish the approaches to landscapes represented by World Heritage Convention Cultural Landscapes, the European Landscape Convention and Category V protected areas or Protected Landscapes/Seascapes.

Fig. 10   Three international approaches to landscape

Initiative	Geographical scope of application	Character of landscape affected	Areas covered by the initiative	Main aims
World Heritage Convention Cultural Landscapes	Global	Outstanding universal value	Any appropriate area	Protect heritage values
European Landscape Convention	Europe	All landscapes	Town and country	Protect, manage and plan landscape
Category V protected areas: Protected Landscapes/seascapes	National and sub-national	Landscapes/seascapes that deserve protection	Rural and coastal areas only	Integrate activities and enhance natural and cultural values

3.5.4 Transboundary Protected Landscapes

Finally, some Category V areas will form part of transboundary protected areas. The planner should be aware of the opportunities for collaboration between two or more Category V protected areas across national boundaries. It may be possible to create a genuine partnership between adjoining areas (and communities) in neighbouring countries; or to relate a Category V area on one side of the border to a more strictly protected area on the other side. General advice on the challenging issues raised by transboundary protected areas has been published by IUCN (Sandwith *et al.*, 2001), and is as relevant to Category V as it is to other kinds of protected area. A recent analysis identified 42 transboundary protected area complexes in which one or more Category V protected areas were included (Zbicz, 2001). **Examples** include:

- France (Mercantour National Park, V) *and* Italy (Alpi Maritime National Park, II);

- Poland (five protected areas, including Doliny Sanu Landscape Park, V, and Tsisniany-Vetliny Landscape Park, V); Slovakia (three protected areas, including Vychodne Karpaty Protected Landscape Area, V); *and* Ukraine (four protected areas, including Nadsan'ski Regional Landscape Park, V);

- Canada (Roosevelt International Park, V), *and* USA (Campobello National Monument, V); and

- Colombia (Catatumbo-Bari Natural National Park, II) *and* Venezuela (two protected areas, including Région Lago de Maracaibo – Sierra de Perijá Protected Zone, V).

Case study 5 shows the potential for international co-operation offered by transboundary Protected Landscapes.

CASE STUDY 5
Champlain-Richelieu Valley, USA and Canada – working across a national boundary

The Champlain-Richelieu Valley (Quebec, Canada; Vermont and New York, USA) has been shaped over two centuries by farming, forestry and transportation along its waterways. The landscapes and historic sites of this transboundary region record a formative part of the history of the US and Canada, and of relationships among early French and English explorers and settlers, First Nations peoples, and the natural landscape (Drost, 2001).

Much of the land is still under agriculture, mostly small dairy farms; tourism is also important to the local economy, especially near the region's lakes. Most people live in small towns and villages. The largest settlement, Burlington (Vermont) strives to be a model of sustainability, with a programme to achieve many of the aims of Agenda 21.

The Champlain-Richelieu Valley is currently being considered for designation in the US as a National Heritage Area, and as a comparable designation in Canada. On the US side, workshops and public meetings have been held around the region to obtain public input and comments from all stakeholders. A parallel process is underway in Québec.

There are institutional and political barriers to designation and an effective management plan. There is some resistance to governmental designation, and there is a language challenge. But experience in the Champlain-Richelieu region demonstrates that public participation can help build local support for designation, enhance communication and foster mutual understanding among diverse communities across political boundaries. The process of designation of an international heritage area provides an important opportunity to test the Category V approach in a US and Canadian context, where a Category II protected area would be likely to meet strong

Cont.

CASE STUDY 5
Champlain-Richelieu Valley, USA and Canada – working across a national boundary (cont.)

local resistance (c.f the reaction to the nearby Adirondack State Park in New York). Communities and residents have been ready to engage in voluntary approaches to protect natural and cultural resources, including private land conservation (e.g. conservation easements and agricultural preservation restrictions) and public-private partnerships.

Source: Jessica Brown (see also Drost, 2000)

3.6 Boundaries for Category V protected areas

From the foregoing, it will be clear that it is important that the boundaries of a Category V protected area should be considered as "permeable". As with all protected areas, Protected Landscapes should not be treated as islands apart from the area around. Rather, it is essential to strengthen many of the links which they have to their surroundings, and specifically to other protected areas (see above). This is best done if the Category V area forms an integral part of a regional approach to conservation and sustainable development.

Nonetheless, all protected areas involve the geographically-focused operation of special policies: so it follows that the establishment of a protected area of any kind requires the delimitation of its boundaries. The drawing of appropriate boundaries for Category V protected areas is critical to its subsequent success, but note that in two ways boundary-drawing for Category V protected areas poses special challenges:

- they require that particular attention be paid to the social aspects (the sense of community identity, for example), thus making this exercise more than a relatively simple matter of mapping and interpreting natural phenomena. In many cases the local community is itself a source of knowledge that should be directly involved in drawing up recommended boundaries; and
- the boundary of Category V protected areas should hardly ever be thought of as a sharp barrier between areas of different quality – in most situations it will be based on an easily identifiable feature within a zone of transition.

Box 8. *Guidelines* for determining the boundaries of a Category V protected area

The following factors should be taken into account in determining the broad extent of the area to be designated:

- Include the totality of the area – the boundary should be drawn to encompass the entire area with a distinctive character which deserves protection. Include any inland water body, and – in the case of coastal areas – include coastal, estuarine, reef and off shore areas that are ecologically linked to the main land area. Though 'exclaves' – that is isolated islands of designated land of similar character outside the main area – may occasionally be appropriate, the administrative complications of this arrangement should be recognised;

Cont.

Box 8. *Guidelines* **for determining the boundaries of a Category V protected area (cont.)**

- Ensure the integrity of the area – the boundary should generally exclude areas which diminish significantly the integrity of the landscape. However, the establishment of 'enclaves' – that is holes of non-designated land, e.g. to accommodate a mine – should be approached with caution: it may be better to have the problem contained within the protected area and thus subject to more influence and control (but see also below);
- Areas to be included may be of differing landscape character; quality rather than uniformity should be the key determinant;
- Boundaries should facilitate effective planning, management and environmental monitoring;
- Consider cultural as well as natural factors. The sense of community identity should be "mapped" and taken into account. This is a powerful argument for the involvement of local people in the boundary-drawing exercise;
- Include settlements that contribute to the rural economy and community life; exclude those where urban and/or industrial development conflicts with, or outweighs the essential value of the area as a whole;
- Protect the people/nature link – the boundary should take into account not only the distinctive nature of the landscape, but also the functional connections (especially those of economy and livelihood), and the non-material associations which the human community has with it;
- Take account of both present land uses and future commitments – for example, an area with a mining permit over it, or with important mineral potential, may need to be excluded, even if work has not yet taken place; and
- Consider the areas around – special measures may be needed in the surrounding areas to ensure that the aims of the protected area can be secured (including establishing a buffer zone).

The following factors should be taken into account at the stage of determining the detailed alignment of the boundary (clearly they may have conflicting implications):

- The importance of a physical boundary that can be easily recognised on the ground (e.g. a natural feature, like a river or a mountain watershed; or an artificial one, like a road);
- The need to avoid splitting human settlements, or dividing a community from its land; and
- The practical benefits of "sharing" the boundary of the Category V protected area with other administrative boundaries, e.g. those of a commune or other local authority unit.

Once agreed upon, it is desirable that the boundary should be appropriately marked on the ground, for example with roadside or trail-side markers, at key access points.

Box 8 sets out suggested guidelines to be followed in defining the boundaries.

Finally legislation should include arrangements for adjusting the boundary in the light of experience. Such flexibility will be important, as circumstances will change over time (for example, the construction of a new road may make an established boundary inappropriate). In principle, procedures for modifying boundaries should be no less rigorous than those used to define boundaries in the first place.

3.7 Involvement of local communities and other stakeholders

Many of the general points made below on stakeholder participation in the management policies (Section 5.2) and especially in the management processes (Chapter 6) for Protected Landscapes are also relevant at the planning stage – see also Figure 10.

Different kinds of stakeholders will emerge at different levels during the planning phase, and their appropriate involvement is essential at each. Thus at the national level, a government, embarking on the development of a network of Category V protected areas as part of its national system of protected areas (see 3.3 above), should consult widely with national sources of expertise, and national groups representative of local interests. Where a regional scale of governance exists, the emphasis will often be more on economic factors. Involvement of stakeholders is especially important at the local scale: in fact, it is never too soon to involve local communities in the planning of a Category V protected area, certainly well before the area is established[4]. Indeed, there may be cases where the impetus to create a Category V protected area comes not from government at all, but from a community or coalition of local groups. Box 9 gives guidance on stakeholder involvement at each level.

Based on experience from the insular Caribbean, Geoghegan and Renard (2002) suggest four key messages on community involvement in planning and management of protected areas:

   ▪ Effective management requires the integration of the full diversity of stakeholders and takes into account the differing ways they are impacted by and impact upon protected areas;

   ▪ The long-term success of participatory management depends on the suitability of the institutional arrangements;

   ▪ Given the limited resources available for protected area management, transparent processes of negotiation are required to determine how much participation is possible and what objectives are given priority; and

   ▪ Participatory management of protected areas must yield appreciable benefits for local communities.

Efforts to foster community participation must take into account the diversity of stakeholder interests, which are determined by factors including gender, age, social class and cultural capital. While some stakeholders are prominent and easily identifiable, others tend to be forgotten or ignored. Participatory protected area planning and management processes must seek to ensure their involvement. These processes must be flexible enough to respond to, and integrate change, because resource use patterns, institutions and power relations are in constant evolution (Geoghegan and Renard, 2002).

Approaches to planning and management in Category V protected areas should also be sensitive to the gender equity perspective. This is more than "women's activities for

---

[4] Note that in some cases it may be the practice to prepare the management plan <u>before</u> the Category V protected area is established (see section 6.2), in which case consultation around the preparation of the plan can be used to achieve stakeholder participation in the designation of the area.

women". Instead it requires a recognition that in many societies there are unequal power relations between genders, and that this calls for actions that involve both women and men in building a participatory and equitable approach to conservation and sustainable development. The principles underlying gender equity in protected areas have recently been promoted by IUCN/WCPA (Aguilar *et al.*, 2002).

Box 9. *Guidelines* on involving stakeholders in planning at national, regional and local levels

National level

In preparing a national programme for the establishment of Category V protected areas, the following sources of expertise should be consulted:

- National arms of government, notably those with responsibilities for biodiversity conservation, protection of the cultural and built heritage, agriculture, transport, tourism, natural resources (e.g. water, soils, forests), and rural, community and regional development;
- National academies of science and equivalent bodies with expert knowledge of landscape, the cultural and built heritage, biodiversity, genetic materials (including that of crops and livestock), geography, agriculture, natural resources, anthropology, ethnography and archaeology; and
- National NGOs and similar representatives of civil society, with interests in the conservation of nature, landscape, the cultural and built heritage, rural development etc.

Regional level (N.B. it is recognised that a regional level of government is missing in many parts of the world)

The integration of Category V protected areas into regional development requires that these interests in particular be consulted:

- Regional economic development agencies;
- Regional nature conservation agencies;
- Regional environmental protection agencies, lobby groups etc.;
- Regional land use planning bodies;
- Regional tourism development agencies; and
- Regional arms of government.

Local level

Category V protected areas are lived-in, working landscapes. Therefore the "people" dimension of their planning assumes an even greater significance than is usually the case with protected areas. There should always be comprehensive public engagement and dialogue on the proposal to establish such an area, its powers, boundaries etc. In particular, the involvement of local interests should begin right at the outset of the planning stage, as part of the process of identifying suitable places for the establishment of Category V protected areas. The principal interest groups whose involvement is needed are:

- Local government bodies within the area;

Cont.

Box 9. *Guidelines* on involving stakeholders in planning at national, regional and local levels (cont.)

Other community leaders, e.g. village headmen, priests, parish/commune leaders;

Resource users: e.g. farmers, graziers, foresters, fishers, miners – and their representatives;

Those with rights in the area: e.g. indigenous peoples, landowners, commoners – and their representatives;

Those with an economic interest: e.g. hoteliers, shopkeepers, transport operators – and their representatives, such as local chambers of commerce (N.B. resource users, those with rights and those with an economic interest are not always exactly the same people);

Those representing other relevant interests, e.g. women's groups, local conservation or human rights NGOs; and

Those individuals with knowledge relevant to the area, e.g. holders of traditional knowledge on land use practices and associated customs, historians, artists and scientists.

3.8 Building public and political support

All protected areas require public support and political backing if they are to succeed. It is true that many people have an interest in Protected Landscapes: city dwellers, tourists and others are also potential stakeholders, for example, and they can generate political support for the aims of the area. But the key factor is that Category V protected areas are lived in: most such areas have a local electorate, and the people living within them are therefore represented by locally-elected representatives or others who speak for the community. The support of such opinion leaders is vital; they in turn will respond to local enthusiasms and concerns.

Therefore these Guidelines stress throughout the need for stakeholder participation and involvement of local people at every stage of the planning and management process. This is not only to build an understanding among the community of the aims of protected area, but also to engage their knowledge and secure their involvement in its management. Local people should be treated as partners, their views carefully considered and their support never taken for granted.

But public and political support will only be guaranteed when local people can see a connection between the protected area and their livelihoods. This does not mean that every economic aspiration can be met, and there are bound to be 'losers' as well as 'winners'. It is therefore important that at the planning stage the potential economic, social and environmental implications of creating a Category V protected area are fully explained, and the constraints that will follow from establishment are honestly faced up to. But the potential benefits should be set out too. Since Category V protected areas usually involve developing support for the traditional economic and cultural practices of the community concerned, it should normally be possible to develop a broad body of public and political support for designation. Often, though, local people will be suspicious of arguments that are not backed by hard evidence, hence the importance of the growing number of success stories about Category V protected areas from around the world, as set out in the case studies in this – and associated – publications.

4. Management of Category V protected areas: Principles

4.1 General principles of protected area management

"Management" is used here to mean the process by which policies and objectives for established Category V protected areas are agreed upon, set out, implemented, monitored and reviewed.

As a general rule, management should:

- be based on principles (Chapter 4);
- deliver action across a range of policies (Chapter 5);
- incorporate appropriate processes and plans (Chapter 6); and
- be implemented through appropriate institutional, financial and other means (Chapter 7).

4.2 Twelve principles for the management of Category V protected areas

The following twelve principles apply **in particular** to the management of Category V protected areas. While some of these may also apply in other protected area situations, for example where a more strictly protected area is under a co-management regime (see Box 29), they take on an added significance in the management of Protected Landscapes.

Principle 1:
Conserving landscape, biodiversity and cultural values are at the heart of the Category V protected area approach. Though much emphasis is placed in this guidance on economic and social considerations, Category V is a conservation approach which should reflect the over-arching objectives of all protected areas as indicated in the definition in Section 2.2.3 above. It is therefore about managing change in such a way that environmental and cultural values endure: change should take place within limits that will not disrupt those values.

Principle 2:
*The focus of management should be on the **point of interaction** between people and nature.* To recall part of the definition used in the 1994 Guidelines: "Safeguarding the integrity of (the) traditional interaction is vital to the protection, maintenance and evolution of the area" (IUCN, 1994, p.22). Thus, whereas in many other kinds of protected areas it is nature itself that is the main focus of management, what distinguishes Category V is that management primarily addresses the **linkage** between people and nature.

Principle 3:
People should be seen as stewards of the landscape. As the occupants of lived-in, working landscapes that are of great value to society as whole, the people living within

Category V protected areas should be supported in their role as stewards of the landscape. They are the architects of much that we value in the landscape, and their support is needed to ensure its survival. Ideally, they help to shape and care for the environment with the traditions of the past, but with an eye to the future. In that sense, they may more correctly be described as 'the managers' of Protected Landscapes than the professionals who are employed with that formal title: good managers in the professional sense will therefore see their role as 'facilitators' and negotiators'.

Principle 4:

Management must be undertaken **with** *and* **through** *local people, and mainly* **for** *and* **by** *them.* This principle recognises that the full involvement of local people is essential, and that Category V protected areas should never be planned **against** their long-term interests. It also recognises that local communities should play an important role in delivering protected area objectives and be among the principal beneficiaries of these. But note that local people are not the only source of expertise. Moreover, there are other stakeholders who can derive benefits from protected landscapes: for example, visitors from nearby urban areas or further afield, resource users from afar (e.g. consumers of water supplies downstream), or the wider community interested in biodiversity or landscape protection.

Principle 5:

Management should be based on co-operative approaches, such as co-management and multi-stakeholder equity. It follows from Principles 2–4 that structures and processes are needed to ensure that people are involved fully in shaping management decisions and come to see the protected area as theirs. This will require the operation of open, transparent procedures based on democratic principles. Co-management approaches may be particularly appropriate to Category V protected areas (see Box 29).

Principle 6:

Effective management requires a supportive political and economic environment. The foregoing principles cannot be followed unless broader governance structures and practices in society at large are committed to certain standards. The management of Protected Landscapes will be easier to achieve if the government recognises the need for a quality of life perspective, follows democratic processes, and engages willingly in participatory planning based upon a fair and equitable approach to all groups and respect for a plurality of cultures. It will also be greatly helped by a top-level national commitment to sustainability, the alleviation of poverty, addressing the root causes of inequality, promoting gender equity and supporting civil society.

Principle 7:

Management of Category V protected areas should not only be concerned with protection but also enhancement. Because Category V protected areas are lived-in landscapes, the environment will have been manipulated more than is the case with other categories of protected areas. It follows that a more active role for management is appropriate, not only in the protection but also in restoration of natural or cultural values that have been eroded or lost. It may on occasion also include the creation of new environmental and social assets which are ecologically or culturally appropriate: examples would be a new woodland or forested areas established on degraded soils, and the development of a new market for goods produced by local people.

Principle 8:

When there is an irreconcilable conflict between the objectives of management, priority should be given to retaining the special qualities of the area. Because Protected Landscapes have important social as well as environmental objectives, there is considerable potential for conflict between objectives. As far as possible, management should seek to reconcile such conflicts. In the last analysis there need to be clear rules about what would have priority in such a situation. This principle states that when this happens, priority should be given to protecting the qualities that make the area special (what economists sometimes call 'critical environmental capital'). Because such a claim is likely to be contested, the principle may need to be embodied in legislation.

Principle 9:

Economic activities that do not need to take place within the Protected Landscape should be located outside it. As a lived-in, working landscape, a Category V protected area will contain a variety of economic activities and land uses, such as agriculture, forestry, tourism and some forms of industry, commerce and retailing, as well as residential areas, some infrastructure, etc. The tests for whether such an activity or use is acceptable within the protected area, are whether (i) it is sustainable, (ii) it contributes to the aims of the area, and (iii) there are strong reasons for it to be located within it. Where the proposed activity fails these tests, it should either be totally re-designed to fit Category V objectives or located outside the area altogether.

Principle 10:

Management should be business-like and of the highest professional standard. Notwithstanding the strong social and environmental emphasis in the management of Protected Landscapes, the operation of management should be business-like, and hardheaded if necessary. It requires effective marketing of conservation approaches too. While this may be difficult to achieve in the short term, financial sustainability should be an aim, rather than 100% reliance on public funding[1]. Procedures should be put in place to ensure that public, private and voluntary funds and other resources are used with due regard to economy, efficiency and effectiveness. And all decision-making concerning the use of resources should be transparent and accountable.

Principle 11:

Management should be flexible and adaptive. Like protected area management in general, that of Category V protected areas needs to be capable of adjustment over time in light of experience and changing circumstances – but since its scope embraces both natural and human systems, the need for flexibility is all the greater. Management of Protected Landscapes should also be flexible and adaptive in the sense that it should respond to the very different social, cultural and economic situations in which it takes place: it should always be culturally appropriate and economically relevant.

Principle 12:

*The success of management should be measured in environmental **and** social terms.* Though absolutely central, biodiversity measures are only one of several indicators: others include social and economic welfare and the quality of life for local and other people, other environmental considerations such as energy efficiency or natural resource management, and measures relating to the conservation of the cultural environment. An

---

[1] See especially WCPA Economics Task Force, 2000. *Financing Protected Areas: Guidelines for Protected Area Managers*, IUCN Gland, Switzerland and Cambridge, UK.

aim should be to demonstrate the maximum social and economic benefits for the local community with the minimum environmental impact. The setting of objectives, allocation of resources and monitoring of effectiveness should all be undertaken with this breadth of interest in mind[2].

---

[2] For further guidance see: Hockings M., Stolton S. and Dudley N. 2000. *Evaluating Effectiveness: A Framework for Assessing the Management of Protected Areas*, IUCN, Gland, Switzerland and Cambridge, UK.

5. Management of Category V protected areas: Policies

5.1 General objectives for the management of Category V protected areas

The starting point for the development of management policies is the list of objectives for Category V protected areas, as set down in the 1994 guidance on protected area management categories – see Box 10.

Box 10. Objectives of management for Category V protected areas

The following objectives of management for Protected Landscapes/Seascapes are set out in the Guidelines for Protected Area Management Categories (IUCN, 1994):

- to maintain the harmonious interaction of nature and culture through the protection of landscape and/or seascape and the continuation of traditional land uses, building practices and social and cultural manifestations;

- to support lifestyles and economic activities which are in harmony with nature and the preservation of the social and cultural fabric of the communities concerned;

- to maintain the diversity of landscape and habitat, and of associated species and ecosystems;

- to eliminate where necessary, and thereafter prevent, land uses and activities which are inappropriate in scale and/or character;

- to provide opportunities for public enjoyment through recreation and tourism appropriate in type and scale to the essential qualities of the areas;

- to encourage scientific and educational activities which will contribute to the long term well-being of resident populations and to the development of public support for the environmental protection of such areas; and

- to bring benefits to, and contribute to the welfare of, the local community though the provision of natural products (such as forest and fisheries products) and services (such as clean water or income derived from sustainable forms of tourism).

These objectives remain relevant, but there have been some significant developments since 1994, both in the understanding of Category V protected areas and in the broad context within which protected areas are managed (see also Section 2.5 above). The most important have been these:

- the importance now attached to full stakeholder involvement in the management of protected areas of all kinds, but especially of those that are the homes and workplaces of people;

43

a fuller understanding of how Category V protected areas can contribute to conservation and sustainable development at the bio-regional scale, both in relation to other protected areas and to rural areas at large;

a growing appreciation that Category V protected areas can be suitable places for integrated and sustainable rural development;

greater recognition of the value of the genetic material contained in domesticated crops and livestock found in many Protected Landscapes;

more emphasis on the non-material values of many landscapes associated with the traditions and human use of these areas.

In light of these, the list in Box 10 needs to be amplified with some additional objectives of management, see Box 11.

Box 11. Additional objectives of management for Category V protected areas

In light of developments since 1994, the following additional objectives for management of Protected Landscapes/Seascapes are suggested:

to provide a framework which will underpin community participation in the management of valued landscapes or seascapes and the natural resources and heritage values that they contain;

to contribute to bio-regional scale conservation and sustainable development;

to buffer and link more strictly protected areas;

to encourage the understanding and conservation of the genetic material contained in domesticated crops and livestock;

to help ensure that the associative and non-material values of the landscape and traditional land use practices are recognised and respected; and

to act as models of sustainability, both for the purposes of the people and the area, so that lessons can be learnt for wider application.

The remainder of this chapter considers the principal policy areas that normally need to be addressed in the management of Category V protected areas, illustrates these with case studies and sets out a number of recommended guidelines. Though, for convenience, the sections treat each policy area separately, **it is a fundamental requirement of a sustainable approach that the policies should be developed and implemented in an integrated way**. The impact of the whole suite of Protected Landscape policies should therefore be much more than the sum of their parts. Each policy area should reinforce another – for example, support for traditional forms of agriculture should help protect biodiversity, assist tourism, underpin the local economy and sustain the community.

5.2 Policies relating to the role of local people

"Local people" in the case of Category V protected areas are normally those communities that live within or use the protected area, though the definition may occasionally include some groups who do not permanently occupy the territory (for example, mobile peoples that move over distances in pursuit of their lifestyles[1]). The important point is that the groups considered are those whose livelihoods are intimately connected with the landscape, and with its associated natural and cultural values which the designation sets out to protect.

There are conceptual, practical and ethical reasons for putting local people first in drawing up management policies for Category V protected areas, as indeed is implied by several of the basic principles set out in Section 4.2 above. But "putting local people first" does not mean that the environmental and other values of the area should be subordinated to social and economic ones; nor that the views of local peoples must always prevail. Rather it recognises that the survival of these values depends on the support of people, and that such support can only be secured if local people are listened to, and their priorities are – where possible – appropriately addressed in the management policies for the area. Specifically this means: (i) placing the concept of local people as 'stewards' for the Category V protected area at the centre of management planning (5.2.1); (ii) considering the implications of land ownership (5.2.2); and (iii) adopting policies to involve local people in decision-making and management (5.2.3 and 6.2).

5.2.1 Local people as stewards of the Protected Landscape

Though the term has many meanings, in the environmental field 'stewardship' has come to indicate an approach that aims to "create, nurture and enable responsibility in users and owners to manage and protect land and natural resources" (Mitchell and Brown, 1998, see also photo 3). It thus implies the care by individuals of natural resources on behalf of society as a whole, now and in the future, and for other species. It requires that people accept sensible conditions on how property is used, and the need to serve both the private and public interest. There is an ethical dimension to the concept as well (WWF/Scotland, 2001).

In the context of conservation as a whole, stewardship is important because it can include:

  sustaining (or reviving) traditional land or water uses, such as farming and small-scale forestry or coastal fisheries, which are important to ecological, economic and scenic values;

  creating biological corridors, greenways and trails across privately owned or managed land;

  through partnerships, enhancing the ability of government agencies to acquire and manage publicly owned parks and protected areas;

  protecting open space and fragile natural areas in the face of development pressures, especially in areas where planning controls are weak; and

  conserving biodiversity through protection and management of habitats.

Stewardship approaches are particularly relevant to Category V protected areas. This is so because such areas aim to reinforce local responsibility for resource management, build on existing institutional responsibilities, and establish flexible and collaborative arrangements for conservation and sustainable development. Moreover, since Category

---

[1] The special case of mobile peoples and protected areas is the subject of the IUCN-supported Dana Declaration (2002). For the full text of this document, see www.danadeclaration.org.

V protected areas often contain a mosaic of ownerships (see next section), their management requires an approach based in part on private ownership, using partnerships where possible rather than acquisition by public bodies. Also, many Protected Landscapes are working landscapes, shaped by the interaction of people and nature over time: in the face of changing economic and environmental conditions, the need is for a dynamic process of landscape evolution – aiming to sustain its general character, rather than preserve its every detail.

Stewardship meets these needs. It is about how people relate to their environment, and especially about how they discharge their responsibilities over the natural resources in their ownership. Thus it is a suitable unifying theme for the management of Category V protected areas. Reference to it in policies is a means of reminding all concerned that management of resources should be done with a view to the longer term and the broader interest.

Although stewardship approaches depend on co-operation and partnerships between individual landowners, resource users, businesses and NGOs, government (or its agencies) plays a key role, by providing a framework in the form of tax and other incentives, land use planning and a supportive climate for private organisations (Brown and Mitchell, 2000). Through voluntary alternatives to controls over changes in land use, construction etc., stewardship mechanisms may offer practical means of achieving the planning policies of a Protected Landscape (e.g. those relating to directing and stimulating development, guiding changes in land use, and providing infrastructure – see also Section 5.4.1).

A number of tools have been developed to promote a stewardship approach. Depending on local contexts, these can include:

- **education and information** on why and how to manage resources in certain ways;
- **recognition** of responsible stewardship, e.g. through award schemes;
- **celebration** of traditional or cultural land use practices supportive of conservation objectives;
- **learning** from the knowledge of local peoples in managing resources;
- formal and informal **agreements** on specific practices, areas of land or projects;
- **incentives** in the form of grants, environmental and social payments, or tax relief;
- **legally binding surrender of rights**, such as in conservation easements (Diehl and Barrett, 1988); and
- gifting or selling **ownership** or control of land.

These tools can be for a limited time (term) or permanent (in perpetuity), but the essential characteristic of all of them is that they are **voluntary** ways of improving land management.

5.2.2 Land tenure

As the 1994 guidance recognises, land and water in Category V protected areas "may be owned by a public authority, but is more likely to comprise a mosaic of private and public ownerships operating a variety of management regimes" (IUCN, 1994, page 22).

Here again, Category V differs in degree from all other protected areas. Whilst many protected areas in other categories contain privately-owned areas, and some indeed are entirely privately- or community-owned, few will display the number and variety of owners which characterise a Protected Landscape. Typically, areas of land and water within a Category V protected area may be owned by:

- The managing authority for the protected area;
- The central government, and its ministries and agencies (including those responsible for forestry, defence, water, energy and transport);
- Regional and local government, and their agencies;
- Local communities;
- Indigenous peoples and traditional owners;
- Private owners of all kinds:
  - individual resource users, like farmers, foresters, fishers,
  - commercial exploiters of natural resources, like quarries and mines, forestry companies,
  - service trades like caterers and hotel keepers,
  - business and industry,
  - community groups,
  - other residents;
- Conservation NGOs (e.g. Land Trusts), whose interests may be in biodiversity, landscape, the historic heritage, living culture and/or public access;
- Religious institutions;
- Universities and schools; and
- Other institutions like co-operatives, land-owning charities and investment companies.

The position may be further complicated by the presence of various kinds of rented and other temporarily occupied property, so that owners and occupiers are often different people.

In some countries, political change has been accompanied by large-scale alterations in the pattern of land tenure. Examples are privatisation of land formerly held by the State (e.g. in former Soviet-bloc countries), and land reform programmes in countries where large estates were formerly privately owned (e.g. in parts of Africa and Latin America). Such trends are extending private land ownership.

5.2.3 Partnerships

It follows from the above, that the management of a Category V protected area requires a major investment in working with and through the many different owners and interests, each with their respective rights. Restraint over the exercise of rights associated with land ownership is often a sensitive matter and, in this respect at least, the management challenge is far more formidable than that which faces the manager of most other kinds of protected area where public ownership is usually more extensive. On the other hand, the Category V approach offers the potential to build collaborative partnerships between the protected area agency, the private landowner and resource user, and the local community. Such partnerships should be based on a shared agenda, rather than the agency adopting a generally negative and restrictive role towards those owning land or exercising other legal interests in the protected area.

CASE STUDY 6.
National Capital Greenbelt, Ottawa, Canada – landscape protection through partnership

The National Capital Greenbelt is a 20,000 ha greenspace and rural landscape that surrounds Canada's capital, Ottawa, to the south of the Ottawa River. It comprises a rural landscape consisting of farmland, forests, wetlands, recreational open space, small rural communities, and land used by public and private institutions. Although the National Capital Greenbelt is publicly owned, its success in protecting a rural landscape adjacent to a large metropolitan area is largely due to collaborative partnerships between the National Capital Commission (NCC, a Federal Crown Corporation) and a variety of other institutions and interests. This collaboration is evident in several ways:

> Protection of the Greenbelt is primarily pursued by implementing a Greenbelt Master Plan (1996) that was developed through an open process involving all levels of government, the general public, and specific interest groups;
>
> Although the NCC is not subject to the laws and requirements of lower levels of government, the NCC complies from a policy perspective. The planning and management of the Greenbelt is a partnership involving federal, provincial and municipal levels of government. Land-use planning provisions mirror the NCC policy for the Greenbelt;
>
> The NCC, as the dominant landowner within the Greenbelt, encourages its tenant farmers to follow best management practices and promotes sustainable forestry; and
>
> Protection of significant natural and cultural heritage resources within the Greenbelt, including a Ramsar site and a provincial historic site, depend on partnerships with relevant stakeholders.

Source: Guy Swinnerton

CASE STUDY 7.
Amboseli/Longido Heartlands, Kenya/Tanzania – a community partnership for conservation and sustainable development

The area includes six large ranches in Kenya near Amboseli National Park and, in adjoining Tanzania, the slopes of Mt. Kilimanjaro and the savannahs of Longido. Some 56 mammal species and 400 species of birds inhabit the area. The Maasai, who are pastoralist people, have lived here for over 400 years, co-existing with the wildlife in relative harmony. The local communities are involved at all levels of management in a range of conservation and enterprise development initiatives,

Cont.

CASE STUDY 7.
Amboseli/Longido Heartlands, Kenya/Tanzania – a community partnership for conservation and sustainable development (cont.)

especially the Maasai-owned tourism-related businesses. As they began to participate in conservation activities, they have developed 'Morani' Cultural homesteads. Tourism helps sustain traditional jobs, such as craft production, while craft co-operatives have been established to cater for tourists visiting these homesteads. Villagers have organised themselves by setting up management structures to implement wildlife policy, conduct training in leadership negotiations, carry out game scouting, raise and manage funds, and make agreements with private companies. The local people are thus developing alternative income sources which do not threaten to deplete the flora and fauna of the protected areas. This helps to maintain the Maasai culture and traditions in terms of how they live, work, dress and interact – while livestock keeping remains the major activity. The result of this supportive policy and planning framework, developed by and through local people, is a 'wildlife-friendly' range. This adjoins neighbouring parks, and – by providing a wider rangeland for park wildlife – takes some of the pressures off them.

Source: Bob Wishitemi

There is no one, single recipe for achieving co-operation with so many disparate land-owning and other interests but the importance of earlier messages about stakeholder participation is underlined. Also the protected area manager should commit seriously to a partnership approach in which public, private and community interests seek common ground and work together to achieve the objectives of the protected landscape. Case Studies 6 and 7 are examples of such partnerships. Guidelines for building partnerships between different landowners and other interests are suggested in Box 12.

Box 12. *Guidelines* for building partnerships between different landowners and other interests

Protected area managers need to build partnerships between different owners of land and other interests. The following general approach is recommended in going about this:

  First, understand the pattern of land-ownership, tenure rights and other interests within the area (this is information that should be gathered and mapped during the planning stage);

  Then obtain a full understanding of the aims and needs of the partners;

  Next, work with partners, build alliances and identify shared interests and common ground;

  Seek out those partners with resources and willingness to take positive action in support of the aims of the Category V protected area;

  Forge agreements that commit all parties to a programme of work, with technical and financial support where necessary, and with arrangements to keep its implementation under review;

Cont.

Box 12. *Guidelines* **for building partnerships between different landowners and other interests (cont.)**

- Demonstrate how partnerships can benefit all parties, e.g. they can enable the management agency to act as a 'buffer' between the owner and tourists visiting his/her land;

- Consider the scope to develop voluntary Codes of Practice or "Charters" with key interest groups, which set standards for their performance within the protected landscape;

- Ensure that the benefits of partnerships are shared equitably between all the partners;

- Engage in the decision-making in an open and transparent manner to build trust; and

- Invest time and resources to develop action through consensus.

CASE STUDY 8.
Conservation areas in the South Pacific Islands – a community-based approach

In the South Pacific Islands, over 80% of the land area is under customary ownership and managed by communities according to communal ownership values maintained over many generations. On most islands, communal lands can never be sold. They are generally richer in biological diversity than government lands.

Recognising the problems facing conventional national parks in the region, the South Pacific Biodiversity Conservation Programme (SPBCP) was launched in 1993 by the intergovernmental conservation agency, South Pacific Regional Environmental Programme (SPREP). SPBCP's focus on communal lands and the involvement of customary owners and community leaders recognises that *"if you want to do something about biodiversity conservation, you have to work with customary owners"*.

All the island countries were invited to propose conservation areas for support. Selection criteria included three essentials:

1. the area must contain significant examples of one or more ecosystems of global concern;

2. the project must be achievable, with a high level of commitment by landowners, residents and resource users; and

3. the area must be large enough to include a wide range of interactions among local people and natural resources.

Some 20 Community Conservation Area projects have been supported under the programme, in 12 of the 14 island countries. Each area is managed by a co-ordinating committee of local residents, assisted by a Conservation Area Support Officer provided by SPREP. These officers are recruited from the local community and work under the direction of the local committees. They listen to the needs and concerns of the local people, strengthen local institutions, help communities to access resources, and link communities and government.

Cont.

CASE STUDY 8.
Conservation areas in the South Pacific islands – a community-based approach (cont.)

In each country where SPBCP is active, the governments have accepted the approach and use this model for communal land management. By building on traditional land ties and developing the stewardship ethic, this programme offers long-term support for biodiversity conservation and sustainable development in the South Pacific Islands.

Source: Mike Beresford (see also Tuxill (ed.), 2000)

CASE STUDY 9.
Gobi Gurvan Saikhan National Park, Mongolia – a community management area (see photos 6 and 17)

Gobi Gurvan Saikhan National Park (GGSNP) in Mongolia's Southern Gobi Region, was gazetted in 1993 to protect unique desert and desert-steppe ecosystems, globally endangered wildlife (snow leopard), endemic flora, and significant fossil and prehistoric sites. It represents a cultural landscape managed by nomadic live-stock herders for thousands of years.

Livestock herding is by far the most important source of rural livelihoods, gener-ating 30% of the GNP. However Mongolia is also committed to an ambitious protected area target of 30% of its territory. The non-exclusionary National Park concept adopted at GGSNP reflects an attempt to reconcile the herders' need for resource access with conservation aims. The dryland ecosystem of the Gobi, scarce resources and immature central government institutions for PA management, and wide ranging resource management rights given to local governments make manage-ment by local and community institutions an obvious choice.

Since 1998, local communities of GGSNP have organised themselves to develop sustainable livelihoods and protect natural resources. Customary institutions have adapted to socio-economic and political changes, and are now becoming empowered partners in co-management, and a driving force for local conservation and develop-ment initiatives. An innovative community management area includes all zones of the park. Community-based, natural resource management models for pasture, wildlife, tourism and medicinal plants have been developed in several districts. Effective exchange and dissemination of experiences have taken place between communities.

Models pioneered in GGSNP are relevant to national policy development and land reform elsewhere. By applying the principles of equity and recognising the rights and capacity of local communities to manage their own resources, the Gobi experience contributes to an understanding of common property management and of the role of mobile peoples in the conservation of drylands. It also offers a new paradigm for PA management.

Source: Sabine Schmidt

5.2.4 Involving local people in decision-making and management

In recent years, there has been a great deal of much-needed advocacy for the involvement of local people as the principal stakeholders in protected areas and in the management of natural resources (e.g. Borrini-Feyerabend G., ed. 1997, Borrini-Feyerabend *et al.*, 2000, Kothari A. *et al.*, 1997, and Weber R. *et al.*, 2000). Chapter 6 (below) deals with the subject in greater detail: it introduces the concept of co-management, and sets out guidelines for stakeholder involvement in Category V management. In addition, case studies 8 and 9 show how community and stakeholder involvement can operate in practice with reference to a number of Category V or similar areas around the world.

5.2.5 Management implications of making local people a central concern

The economic and cultural wellbeing of local people must be central concerns in the management of Category V protected areas. Thus management should be based on a knowledge of local people, and especially of: their cultural values and beliefs; their economic activities and resource use patterns; their traditional knowledge of sustainable land and natural resource management; and the pressures that they are under. This has implications for managers of protected landscapes, which rarely apply to the same extent in other protected areas:

> it is just as important to build up a detailed knowledge base about the people living in the area as it is about its natural and other values. Data are needed on: population distribution and trends; the aspirations of local people; economic activities and trends; land-related cultural traditions and practices (e.g. those associated with the planting and harvesting of crops); and the area's economic and other forms of dependence on adjoining areas, including cities;

> local people in a Category V protected area are likely to be a more heterogeneous group than in most protected areas. They will probably include not only users of wild living resources (hunters, fishers etc.), but also settled groups like farmers, foresters and miners, as well as others engaged in the manufacturing and service sectors of the economy, for example tourist provision, retailing and craft products, and retired people. They may include employees of private and public enterprises that are headquartered outside the area altogether. They may also include wealthy "incomers", such as retired people, home-based workers using IT or long distance commuters who live in the protected area but travel out of it to work. Such groups often have resources and political contacts and influence that can be used for protected area objectives;

> while local people are likely to be the most important stakeholders in Category V protected areas, many groups from outside will also have an interest and should be taken account of in shaping policies. These include:

> > tourists and recreational visitors to the area;

> > neighbouring populations who depend on the area for its resources (e.g. downstream consumers of water supplies);

> > national, regional and local government departments with functional responsibilities affecting the area (for a very wide range of concerns, such as agriculture, forestry, fisheries, education, health, transport and tourism – and much else besides);

52

national and regional public utilities and corporations, service providers etc. with responsibility for resource use (e.g. State forestry service) and infrastructure (e.g. roads and railways) within the area;

private entrepreneurs based outside the area whose economic interests include activities within the area (e.g. hotel chains);

temporary residents (e.g. weekend visitors, owners of holiday homes); and

national and regional environmental and other NGOs concerned with the conservation of the area and the well-being of its people.

While the designation of a Category V protected area is not usually intended primarily as an economic measure, the policies applied to it should as far as possible bring lasting economic benefit. They should do this by encouraging the sustainable use of natural resources, including that of the landscape itself which can be the enduring foundation of tourism. Case Studies 10 and 11 are examples from France and the Caribbean of how policies for a Category V protected area can address the economic and social needs of the local community.

CASE STUDY 10.
The French Regional Nature Parks – integration of economic and social objectives (see photo 2)

Les Parcs Naturels Régionaux emerge from local initiatives and reflect the concerns, problems and opportunities of the local communities. In response to the need for a flexible framework for conservation and development, the regional nature park system was established in 1967. The first park, Saint Amand-Raismes, was created in 1969.

The objectives of the system are:

to conserve the nature and cultural heritage of the area,

to improve employment and social opportunities, and

to make more effective use of the educational and recreational assets of the area.

Regional nature parks are classified as Category V protected areas. They are created as a result of collaboration between a number of local communities (communes), working in close association with the central regional administration in which they are located. Each park must prepare a charter (*une charte*) detailing the management policies and priorities and their cost. Most parks are managed by a *syndicats mixtes* organisation, consisting of representatives from the communes, public bodies, chambers of trade and commerce, and various local social groups. This body is served by an advisory and administration team, the elected members of which are drawn from the communities and the public authorities.

The French regional nature parks are involved in a range of management and improvement schemes including:

development of visitor centres and ecological museums,

recreation areas and field study hostels,

Cont.

CASE STUDY 10.
The French Regional Nature Parks – integration of economic and social objectives (cont.)

- infrastructure improvements,
- construction of workshops for local workers,
- renovation of redundant agricultural buildings for visitors e.g. *gîtes ruraux*; and
- significant efforts to promote the marketing of local products.

In 1982 a French Government Report (Besson Report) strongly commended the regional nature park system as a highly democratic management model, worthy of widespread adoption for the wider French countryside. There are now 40 such parks, including two – Martinique and Guyane – in overseas territories with developing country characteristics.

Source: Mike Beresford

CASE STUDY 11.
Saint Lucia – using protected landscapes as a catalyst for sustainable development in rural communities in Small Island Developing States (SIDS)

The communities of Praslin and Mamiku are located on the east central coast of Saint Lucia, just outside the proposed Praslin Protected Landscape. Since the 18th century, they have depended on fishing and agriculture and today, like most small rural communities in SIDS, they suffer from very high unemployment and underemployment rates.

The area's resources include fringing mangroves, coral reefs, sea grass beds, a delta, offshore islets, a sheltered bay, beaches, coastal cliffs with xerophytic vegetation, fine scenery, and historic and archaeological sites. To help protect these resources, the Saint Lucia National Trust set up a participatory planning process to create a new protected area and build capacity within the local community. The challenges faced included river pollution from garbage disposal, lack of basic toilets, destruction of mangroves, over-dependence on the government for assistance, lack of strong and effective community structures, and the need to negotiate with private landowners.

It is hoped to establish the protected landscape formally in the near future. Already the planning process has achieved:

- a complete inventory and status report on natural and cultural resources;
- a significant reduction in pollution through garbage collection and disposal;
- the elimination of faeces in the mangroves following the installation of basic toilets;
- the establishment of Saint Lucia's longest coastal nature trail and its designation as a Nature Heritage Tourism Site, which has created employment and involves an agreement to share fees earned between landowners and the community;

Cont.

CASE STUDY 11.
Saint Lucia – using protected landscapes as a catalyst for sustainable development in rural communities in Small Island Developing States (SIDS) (cont.)

- the establishment of a private enterprise, Eastern Tours, who hire community people to undertake management functions and guided tours;
- increased environmental awareness;
- training of community groups, and
- increased capacity of these groups to shape their futures.

This case study shows that protected landscapes can be used as a planning tool in SIDS to achieve conservation and sustainable development by promoting a close symbiotic relationship between nature and people.

Source: Giles Romulus

5.3 Policies relating to resource use: Farming, forestry and fisheries

5.3.1 Working through resource users

Resources users – farmers of all kinds, foresters, fishers, miners etc. – play a particularly important, often pivotal role within lived-in, working landscapes. Often they are the principal architects of the landscape. Thus, while in other kinds of protected areas their activities are at best tolerated, and more often resolutely opposed, they are an essential component of Category V protected areas. This section deals with what are normally the main resource uses, farming, forestry and fisheries: policies for extractive resource uses like mining and quarrying are considered under a later section on the control of economic activities.

5.3.2 Farming: principles and guidelines

In many, if not most, Category V protected areas, farming of one kind or another is the most extensive use of land and the principal force in shaping the land. This is true of many areas that are – or could be considered as – Protected Landscapes. Examples (some of which are illustrated by the photographs) are:

- the rice terraces in several parts of East and South East Asia, as well as other irrigation landscapes in many parts of the world;
- the upland grazing farms of Western Europe;
- mixed montane farming in the Himalayas, Alpine and similar mountain regions;
- the olive, vine and fruit Mediterranean farming systems – see photo 9;
- traditional potato cultivation in the Andes;
- mixed farming systems in Eastern USA and Canada;
- livestock grazing systems, such as those of Central Asia (see photo 6), East Europe (see photo 14) and East Africa, which often also function as wildlife reserves alongside national parks;
- the "himas" reserve areas of the Arab world; and
- wetland landscapes in many parts of the world.

CASE STUDY 12.
Island of Öland, Sweden – support for traditional, sustainable agriculture

The southern part of Öland is dominated by a vast limestone pavement, covering 250km^2, which is the single, largest, actively-farmed limestone pavement in the world. Because of the area's exceptional qualities, most of it is under protective guardianship and subject to national and international oversight.

The character of the landscape reflects more than 5000 years of human exploitation, with farming well adapted to the physical constraints of the area. Numerous traces of traditional settlement patterns and land uses still exist, testifying to the legacy of each period of history. The resulting biodiversity values and cultural assets have been recognised as being of such outstanding universal importance, that the Agricultural landscape of Southern Öland was inscribed as a World Heritage Cultural Landscape in 2000. Also 14,000ha are proposed for inclusion in the European Union's Natura 2000 network.

Well-structured, low impact farming respects the land's capabilities and, coupled with current conservation practices, protects and enhances the landscape character and biodiversity of natural ecosystems. The area's high biodiversity values are actively conserved within contemporary farming systems and through the continuation of traditional farming practices. A legal Stewardship Agreement exists between all the relevant stakeholders to sustain this land use pattern. The agreement emerged from a participatory approach promoted by the Swedish Government to encourage sustainable development on the island. It is underpinned with financial support and reinforced with proactive planning and management policies. Together, these enable the integrated management of the area: thus traditional values are protected, but development in the right place and of an appropriate form is encouraged to continue.

Source: Peter Ogden

An outstanding landscape that owes many of its values to a long-standing and sustainable farming system is described in Case Study 12.

From such varied experience, it is possible to distil general advice on the way in which farming should be addressed in policies for Category V protected areas (see Box 13). Farming in Protected Landscapes should be exemplary, demonstrating the highest environmental standards, bringing lasting economic and social benefits, and based on sustainable principles. The need for this is particularly urgent in some Category V protected areas which are agriculturally marginal. Such areas are vulnerable to inappropriate forms of farming – for example, cropping methods that aim at short-term maximisation of yield without regard to the long-term effect on soil or impacts on water quality or biodiversity; the replacement of locally-adapted livestock or crop varieties with commercially-promoted ones; or indeed the abandonment of land altogether and, with the end of farming, the end of biodiversity dependent on it. The principles set out below, and the emphasis on organic farming and local genetic variety, are all designed to encourage food security and economic survival in marginal regions – as well as providing environmental benefits.

1. Jiuzhaigou Scenic Valley, China. *©Adrian Phillips*
Jiuzhaigou is a World Heritage site. Its native Tibetan population farms some of the land around the travertine lakes and waterfalls. Rare species, including the panda, are to be found in the forests above. Tourism is a major management problem in the valley (see Case Study 25).

2. Corsican Regional Nature Park, France. *©Rosie Simpson*
The French Regional Nature Parks are lived-in landscapes. They aim to support the local economy as well as to protect characteristic landscapes. That in Corsica is one of the largest: it includes much fine scenery and has a distinctive culture (see Case Study 10).

Plate 1

3. Marsh-Billings-Rockefeller National Historical Park, Vermont, USA. ©*Adrian Phillips*
This park is the only one in the US system to focus on conservation history and land stewardship. It interprets the historic Marsh-Billings-Rockefeller property, where conservationists George Perkins Marsh, Frederick Billings and Mr and Mrs Laurance S. Rockefeller have each in turn managed the estate as a model of responsible land management.

4. Annapurna Conservation Area, Nepal.
©*Ken Taylor*
Culture and nature in juxtaposition: Annapurna South and Nilgiri form the stunning background to this cultural landscape. The forest in the middle-ground is under threat both from pressures for agricultural land and to cut timber for firewood, including for camping.

Plate 2

5. National Capital Green Belt, Ottawa, Canada. ©*Guy Swinnerton*
The National Capital Greenbelt is a 20,000ha protected greenspace and rural landscape that surrounds Canada's capital, Ottawa, to the south of the Ottawa River (see Case Study 6). Protected landscapes near cities have great value in recreational, educational and land use planning terms.

6. Gobi Gurvan Saikhan National Park, Mongolia. ©*Sabine Schmidt*
Young girl herding small livestock in the Western Beauty Mountains. This represents a cultural landscape managed by nomadic livestock herders for thousands of years, but important also for rare species of wildlife (see Case Study 9).

Plate 3

7. Niagara Escarpment, Ontario, Canada. *©Niagara Escarpment Commission*
The Niagara Escarpment – view of the town of Milton from Rattlesnake Pass. The escarpment is a Protected Landscape near Toronto. It has mixed forest and farmland and is important for biodiversity, history, scenery, recreation, water supply and quarried stone.

8. Isles of Scilly, UK. *©Adrian Phillips*
Some Category V protected areas are Protected Seascapes. This archipelago off the south west tip of England is important for its scenery, biodiversity, archaeology and history, and is protected as an Area of Outstanding Natural Beauty. Its economy is heavily dependent on tourism.

Plate 4

9. Ancient Olive Groves, North Cyprus. ©*Adrian Phillips*
These olive groves are many hundreds of years old. Many are now being abandoned or even felled, as there is thought to be no longer a market for their oil. The challenge is to find a new value for olive products which will ensure the survival of these magnificent veteran trees.

10. Crafts at Dana Nature Reserve, Jordan. ©*Adrian Phillips*
An initiative by Jordan's Royal Society for the Conservation of Nature has promoted the production and marketing of local produce and crafts. Jams, herbs, jewellery and other products are sold to visitors to the nature reserve. This brings income to villagers and helps in the upkeep of the orchards and field system.

Plate 5

11. Annapurna Conservation Area, Nepal. *©Ken Taylor*
This exquisitely engineered cultural landscape scene near Salligan forms part of a popular trekking route, used by people and mule trains. Discarded litter has become a problem, most of it dropped by local people. If litter bins are not an appropriate response in such an environment, can education help?

12. Philippine Rice Terraces. *©Adrian Phillips*
The Ifugao are the architects of the Philippine Rice Terraces – see cover illustration. Their cultural traditions sustain the annual cycle of planting, harvesting and preparing the rice, as well as underpinning the regular tasks of maintaining irrigation channels, repairing the walls of the rice paddies and soil conservation (see Case Study 4).

Plate 6

13. Harvesting reeds, Balkans.
©*Martin Schneider-Jacoby and EUROPARC Federation*
Reed cutting for thatch and other purposes is a traditional land use in wetland areas that favours biodiversity. Lake Prespa, Albania/Greece/Macedonia (Former Yugoslav Republic).

14. Hungarian Grey Cattle, Hortobágy National Park, Hungary.

15. Giant Bustard, Hortobágy National Park, Hungary.
© *Hortobágy National Park*
Rare and endangered species of wildlife often depend for their survival on long established farming practices that are adapted to local conditions, such as grazing with Hungarian Grey Cattle – a traditional breed associated with the grasslands of Hortobágy National Park, Hungary (see Case Study 20).

Plate 7

16. Potato market, Peru. ©*Brent Mitchell*
Numerous varieties of potatoes are grown in Pisac Cusco, Peru. Protected landscapes can be used to ensure the survival of this genetic heritage (see Case Study 16).

17. Gobi Gurvan Saikhan National Park, Mongolia. ©*Sabine Schmidt*
Petroglyphs at Bichigt Khad testify to over two thousand years of human occupation by both sedentary and nomadic peoples (see Case Study 9). Many Category V protected areas are rich in archaeological remains.

Plate 8

Box 13. Principles and *Guidelines* for policy towards farming in Category V protected areas (based on Ogden, 2002)

Five principles, with associated guidelines, are recommended for consideration when developing policy towards farming in Category V protected areas, thus:

Principle	*Guidelines*
1: Maintain the quality of the resource	Maintain or enhance the quality of natural resources used in farming (soil, water, air) through sustainable farming methods, such as non-polluting ways of regulating pests and diseases, nutrient recycling, soil protection and using renewable resources and recycled products; Safeguard natural resources by minimising the use of toxic products, limiting artificial inputs, controlling pollution etc.; Conserve biodiversity and cultural assets within traditional farming systems; Support the survival and use of agricultural biodiversity – and thus maintain the genetic diversity in livestock and crops; Restore/rehabilitate land that has been degraded by non-sustainable farming practices.
2: Manage farmers' relationships with other interests	Wherever possible, build on the traditional knowledge of farmers about the management of their land and other natural resources; Integrate farming with conservation of scenery, biodiversity, historic and cultural assets; Encourage farming to help maintain the distinct identity of different landscapes and communities; Encourage complementary links between farming and other suitable activities on farms (e.g. tourism and forestry); Establish management partnerships with farmers and others to deliver integrated programmes of environmental stewardship; Use such partnerships to increase farmers' awareness of the benefits of sustainable agriculture.
3: Maximise opportunities to support sustainable agriculture	Support or develop systems of advice and extension to promote sustainable farming; Seek access to national and international funds to encourage sustainable approaches to farming through systems of incentives, environmental payments etc.; Recognise and reward outstanding achievements in the field of sustainable farming.
4. Ensure that producers get added value from sustainable farming	Encourage producers to develop and market environmentally-sound products; Build new alliances, e.g. with consumers, the organic farm movement, and purchasers of environmentally-sound foods; Develop supplementary sources of income for farmers from sustainable activities (e.g. tourism, crafts); Develop local markets and thus add to local distinctiveness.
5: Engage in the wider picture	Help farmers to adapt to the changing needs of society in ways that retain their independence; Encourage links between farming and other aspects of the rural economy and society.

57

5.3.3 Farming: tools for sustainability

As implied by Box 13, a major focus of the work of the managing agency for Protected Landscapes will be on encouraging farmers to adopt, or maintain, sustainable farming practices. Basically there are four tools for this:

- Education and awareness raising, and training programmes
- Financial/fiscal incentives
- Market incentives
- Regulation

Education is mainly concerned with raising the awareness of farmers about the importance of sustainable approaches to agriculture – though it can also include protected area managers, in the formal sense, learning from farmers. It deals not only with the protection of the resources upon which farming directly depends (especially soil and water), but also the protection of the natural and cultural assets that depend on farming (e.g. wildlife and historic features). It often involves respecting and encouraging traditional, sustainable practices. While there is value in a science-based, production-oriented extension service that advises farmers, in Category V protected areas especially, this advice should be delivered in order to encourage sustainable agriculture (as in Box 13). Advice of this kind needs to be **practical**. Education and awareness raising for a farming audience is best done by people who have worked as farmers and understand the realities of farming. Case study 13 describes the work of the Farming and Wildlife Advisory Group (FWAG) in the UK, which is a model of this approach.

CASE STUDY 13.
The work of the Farming and Wildlife Advisory Group (UK) – conservation advice to farmers

The Farming and Wildlife Advisory Group (FWAG) is a United Kingdom charity whose objectives are to provide advice to farmers, landowners and other clients on the integration of commercial agricultural practices with the retention and creation of wildlife habitats on their land.

An important strength of FWAG is it is based firmly within the farming community, rather than being an outside initiative. It was created in 1969 by a group of farmers and conservationists, and has since then sought to offer the best technical advice and practical guidance on the enhancement of landscape, heritage and wildlife, and the management of resources, access and recreation through environmentally-responsible farming. It operates through a network of professional advisers, each located in 65 local groups led by a volunteer committee. In 2002 the total paid staff was 141.

FWAG advocates a whole-farm approach, with advice based on a detailed analysis of the wildlife and habitat assets of the total farm environment, as well as information relating to farm operations such as chemicals, waste management and pollution. Following an initial visit which is generally free of charge, fee levels depend on the type of work/advice required. The farmer could expect to receive a detailed report with recommendations for short and long term management.

Cont.

> **CASE STUDY 13.**
> **The work of the Farming and Wildlife Advisory Group (UK) – conservation advice to farmers (cont.)**
>
> FWAG receives core funding from the UK Government at the country and local level but most of its income (65%) derives from non-public sources through fees, membership, donations and corporate sponsorship.
>
> FWAG has developed a website (www.fwag.org.uk) to help share and promote ideas and best practice. The International Exchange does this between countries, using pictures to overcome language barriers.
>
> *Source*: Richard Partington

Financial and fiscal incentives are measures normally operated by public agencies and designed to encourage sustainable farming. These may take several forms, all employing a contractual relationship (normally between the farmer or landowner on the one hand, and the management agency or another conservation body on the other). Examples are:

- capital grants to encourage one-off actions (like tree planting or soil protection);
- annual grants to encourage year-on-year environmental care (like wetland maintenance);
- 'conditionality', under which payment of agricultural production grants depends upon environmental performance;
- fiscal relief, under which taxation of some kind is removed or reduced in return for carrying out conservation practices;
- rent reductions etc., where the landowner (which may be a Land Trust-type body) wishes to encourage sustainable farming; and
- credit schemes.

Within a number of countries, governments operate programmes of support for environmentally-sensitive farming, and these can and should be used to further the purposes of Protected Landscapes. A region-wide programme of this kind is operated within the European Union – see Case study 14. Though this is operated within the framework of the EU's Common Agricultural Policy (CAP), such payments are "de-coupled" from support for agricultural production. Properly designed, therefore, they can bring environmental benefits in Europe without disadvantaging farmers in poorer countries.

Market incentives are ways of creating demand for the products of sustainable forms of farming which are appropriate within Category V protected areas, thus giving added value to the very production processes that help to maintain the landscape. Usually this means developing niche markets, which can be quite separate from providing for the subsistence needs of local people or meeting urban mass market demands for food products. The emphasis in promoting the product is placed, above all, on **quality**; and the targets are tourists, and up-market retail outlets both within and outside the protected area. There are many ways in which niche markets of this kind can be developed and support traditional, environmentally-friendly forms of farming, for example by:

- "branding" traditional products from a distinctive area such as a Protected Landscape so as to strengthen the link in the mind of the consumer between place and product (e.g. goods marketed as "Product of the xxx Protected Landscape");

CASE STUDY 14.
The Agri-Environment Programme of the European Union

The first agri-environment measure at the EU level was Article 19 of Council Regulation 797/85. This authorised Member States to introduce 'special national schemes in environmentally sensitive areas' to subsidise farming practices favourable to the environment. Farmers in these "Article 19" areas throughout the 15 Member States were able, voluntarily, to sign a management agreement which supported those agricultural practices which maintained or enhanced the landscape, wildlife or historic value of the areas. The agreements and associated grants varied according to the characteristics of the area but they normally included restrictions on the use of pesticides, regulations on other land management practices and grants for positive management of such landscape features as hedgerows.

The most recent reforms to the Common Agricultural Policy (CAP)(March 1999) include a new Rural Development Regulation (RDR) (EC Regulation 1257/99) which established rural development as the second 'pillar' of the CAP. The Regulation requires all Member States to draw up single, integrated rural development plans to cover all rural areas. Member States are obliged to implement the agri-environment measures contained in the RDR, but can choose to implement the other measures (such as early retirement and training schemes). Approximately 10% of CAP monies have been allocated to the RDR to be spent on a matching basis, though Member States may add their own funds to supplement this through a process known as 'modulation'.

Agri-environment schemes are being used in support of Category V protected areas across the EU. For example, in England – where £100 million (50% EU funds) is spent annually – the national parks (Category V) have developed partnerships with farmers for environmental protection and enhancement. Agri-environment schemes enhance the environmental value of farming by maintaining practices which generate 'public goods' (e.g. wildlife, heritage, scenery) which the 'market' cannot support. They also encourage agriculture to become more environmentally sustainable.

Source: Kevin Bishop

- creating retail outlets for these products within and beyond the area;
- creating a certification system to ensure that products reach reliably high standards, and are produced using practices which are environmentally acceptable or benign; and
- training local people to produce and prepare products for quality markets.

Though such approaches are probably most advanced in wealthier countries, there are an increasing number of examples being applied in developing countries as well, as is shown by some of the examples in Box 14.

Finally there is **regulation**. There are some agricultural activities, including the use of chemicals and other potentially polluting activities, which can threaten water, air or soil, and where regulations must therefore be put in place to safeguard the environment of the Protected Landscape. This requires enforceable rules based on legally backed standards, regular inspections and spot checks.

Box 14. Innovative marketing of traditional agricultural products

There are a number of examples where innovative marketing is being used to create a demand for products from traditional forms of agriculture and related land use that would be appropriate in Category V protected areas:

>   organic jams and other fruit products are grown and marketed to visitors to the Dana Nature Reserve, Jordan under a local brand (see web site http:// www.rscn.org.jo, and photo 10);

>   top quality rice wine is made from local rice in the Ifugao rice terraces, Philippines (see also Case Study 4);

>   the Export Promotion of Organic Products from Africa Programme (EPOPA) has helped develop organic coffee, cocoa and cotton production and export, (Ugandan farmers participating in these projects earn 25–30% higher prices from their produce than other farmers not accessing the organic market);

>   smallholders in Central America produce shade-grown (and often organically-grown) coffee and cacao, which is marketed as a premium product in the US;

>   game meat products from grazing lands in a number of countries in Eastern and Southern Africa is sold in quality tourist restaurants;

>   spring water is bottled in, and branded as from, the Brecon Beacons and Snowdonia National Parks (Category V) in Wales, UK;

>   organic products are produced from and marketed by the Hohe Tauern National Park, Austria; and

>   a local carpet industry has been encouraged by European Community support, based upon re-introducing traditional sheep grazing to maintain the habitat of the species-rich meadows in the White Carpathian Mountains, Czech Republic.

If the Category V agency does not itself operate the regulations over agriculture, they should make sure that the body responsible for this works closely with it. Recourse to regulations over land management is, however, often a last resort. In general, regulatory controls are most effective as a means of prohibiting undesirable actions (e.g. illegal tree felling). If the aim of management is to encourage positive land use practices (e.g. tree pollarding), regulations are less likely to be successful: it is often better to use one of the preceding techniques. An exception relates to regulations to maintain agreed production standards, for example regulations for this purpose have been applied successfully to organic farming (see next section), e.g. the US Department of Agriculture's National Standards, EU Regulations on organic food and the WHO/FAO *Codex Alimentarius* Guidelines on organically produced foods.

All four of the tools described in this section require an effective support system and a favourable socio-economic environment to operate successfully. For example, success may depend upon a certain level of literacy among farmers or on the existence of a local radio station if messages on sustainable farming are to be put across and understood.

5.3.4 Farming: Organic agriculture

Organic farming relies on locally available resources, depends upon maintaining ecological balances and develops biological processes to their optimum. Increasingly it is seen as a way of adding value to farm produce, as well as minimising the dangers of pollution and threats to human health from pesticides, fungicides, fertilisers etc. It is especially relevant to farm operations in areas that do not lend themselves easily to intensive farming because of the prevailing physical conditions – steep slopes, harsh climate, thin soils, poor drainage etc. Many such farming regions are, of course, to be found in Category V protected areas (or in areas suitable for designation). Managers of such areas should therefore consider what they can do to encourage organic farming as a way of promoting niche markets for goods produced in an environmentally-sound manner in environmentally significant areas. An example of what can be done to promote organic production is illustrated by Case Study 15.

CASE STUDY 15.
Organic agriculture in the regional parks of Tuscany, Italy

This project provides extension services to farmers in organic agriculture in the parks and buffer zones of three Category V protected areas: Parco delle Alpi Apuane, Parco della Maremma, and Parco di Migliarino-San Rossore-Massaciuccoli. It aims to reach a target of 30% conversion of farms within the park administration, and 20% of all farms in the total area. Its three-year budget is over 340,000 Euros.

Organic agriculture helps maintain the agro-ecosystems of the parks, but there is an ageing farming population and some abandonment of land. The initial focus for the project was on farms in the buffer zones. To encourage conversion, extension services have been developed which:

  gather data on technical and legislative aspects;

  visit organic farms and interview organic farmers;

  hold workshops etc. for local entrepreneurs interested in organic activities within the park;

  operate homeopathic veterinary services for livestock farming; and

  develop demonstration plots.

Technical support focuses on conserving and maintaining soil fertility, selecting species and varieties for crop rotation, animal husbandry and organic livestock production techniques. Assistance is also given in marketing organic products (including a quality label), establishing sales outlets in the parks, and helping manage income from sales.

After 20 months, 27% of farms in Parco della Maremma and in the area around had converted to organic production; also 4% of those in Parco di Migliarino and 8.5% in the wider area of Migliarino.

Source: Sue Stolton, adapted from Migliorini, 2000

5.3.5 Agricultural biodiversity

Agricultural biodiversity – that is genetic diversity in livestock and crops – is the result of ecological processes, topographical conditions and human management. In general, farming systems in remoter regions, and in more rugged terrain, have been less subject to 'improvement' through the use of modern varieties. Because these physical characteristics are also a feature of many Protected Landscapes, Category V protected areas tend to be among the last strongholds of rare and endangered domesticated breeds of cattle, sheep, goats, pigs, fowl etc., and varieties of crops, such as cereals, vegetables and fruit. They survive because farming methods in such places are less likely to have succumbed to the use of modern, highly productive varieties. Often too their use is associated with cultural traditions. Therefore, though few – if any – Protected Landscapes have yet been created primarily in order to safeguard such valuable resources, many existing Category V protected areas can be considered as a means of protecting "hot spots" for agri-biodiversity. This means that they could have particular potential application in the centres of agri-biodiversity and important gene pools, e.g. of rice in parts of South and East Asia, cereals in West Asia, fruits etc. in the Mediterranean, and many vegetables in the Andes. Case Study 16 shows how a Category V approach could benefit the people, the genetic resource and the landscape of the Peruvian centre of potatoes.

CASE STUDY 16.
Proposed 'Potato Park', Peru – Protected Landscape to help save plant genetic resources (see photo 16)

There is an urgent need to protect agri-biodiversity and the fragile mountain ecology of the Andes region, through innovative approaches based on the traditional knowledge and skills of the indigenous peoples. Their ecosystem-based management has helped to create and maintain a wide diversity of domesticated and wild plant and animal species.

In Pisac Cusco, Peru, seven Quechua communities are planning to establish a 'Potato Park', i.e. a community-based, agri-biodiversity focused conservation area, managed through an integrated landscape conservation model on Category V protected area lines. The area is a recognised micro-centre of crop diversity for potatoes and other important Andean crops (e.g. Quinoa, Kiwicha, Tarwi, Ollucu, Oca and Mashua). It lies at the heart of the ancient Inca Empire. The aim is to protect and conserve native plant genetic resources – including landraces and wild relatives of domesticated plants and animal species – as well as associated traditional knowledge, important Andean habitats and local cultural heritage.

The Potato Park initiative addresses local concerns for food security, conservation, economy, education, gender equality, intellectual property and indigenous peoples' self-determination. Its main components are (a) developing alternative economic activities (agro-ecotourism, marketing native crops, etc); (b) capacity building in sustainable agriculture and ecosystem management; and (c) the management of local innovations to sustain livelihoods. There is strong emphasis on "learning by doing". The scheme is planned as a pilot for a larger initiative in landscape conservation in the Andes region.

Cont.

CASE STUDY 16.
Proposed 'Potato Park', Peru – Protected Landscape to help save plant genetic resources (see photo 16) (cont.)

Peruvian authorities and institutions, such as the International Potato Center (CIP), recognise the potential innovative value of the scheme. A committee of government and non-governmental institutions is studying legal options for the formal recognition of the Potato Park, and the CIP has agreed with the communities to repatriate potato varieties. Through the initiative, indigenous peoples are learning of their rights to biological resources and of the potential benefits derived from their use. The Potato Park could be a shelter against rapid changes and cultural degradation, and help achieve development that is compatible with native cultural conservation values and sustainable use goals.

Source: Alejandro Argumedo

5.3.6 Forestry

In most types of protected areas, "forests" mean the remaining natural areas under trees. There will be such natural forests ('old growth', ancient, pristine or virgin forests) in many Category V protected areas too, but other kinds of woodland and forests will also be commonplace. Examples are: woodlots, small plantations, community woodlands, hedges and copses, shelter belts, sacred groves and other people-protected woodlands, fragments of riverine or hilltop forests, tree cover maintained for soil conservation or watershed protection – and so forth. So in Category V protected areas, forests and trees play a complex role.

Guidelines for the management of forests and trees in Category V protected areas are set out in Box 15.

However, forestry and woodland policies for the protected area as a whole will need to be broken down to reflect the many different kinds of forests and woodlands which are often found within a Protected Landscape and the values ascribed to them by society. These might be listed under a number of headings, according to the main functions of the treed area and appropriate policies, for example:

- forests/woodlands managed as nature reserves (often called 'micro reserves' in Latin America), where nature protection will have priority;
- commercial forests/woodlands, which are primarily managed for renewable supplies of timber;
- recreational forest/woodlands, which are primarily managed for their recreational value for local people and visitors;
- community forests/woodlands, which are managed primarily to serve the needs of the local community for food, energy and materials;
- forests/woodlands managed as reserves for the sustainable off-take of wild animals, and other non-timber products like honey;
- watershed forests/woodlands, which help to protect water supply (quality and quantity) for downstream communities (within or outside the protected area);

> **Box 15. *Guidelines* for forests, woodlands and trees in Category V protected areas**
>
> *Managers of Category V protected areas should consider adopting policies towards forests, woodlands and trees along these lines:*
>
> identify and protect all remaining old growth, virgin or ancient forests and woodlands;
>
> safeguard all forest and woodlands that play an important part in watershed protection;
>
> encourage the protection and reinstatement of other woodland features in the landscape, such as hedgerows and copses;
>
> promote community links (economic, educational, recreational, spiritual etc.) with woodlands, so that the value of wooded areas is increased;
>
> respect and support forests and woodlands that are retained by the initiative of local communities;
>
> encourage industry which uses woodlands on a sustainable basis (e.g. well-managed charcoal production, small-scale timber production);
>
> promote links between existing woodland areas by new planting so that ecological corridors and landscape features are enhanced;
>
> encourage the multiple use of forests and woodlands, including as sustainable energy sources;
>
> permit the traditional, sustainable use of medicinal herbs, mushrooms, aromatic plants and wild fruits and vegetables;
>
> add value to forest products by processing them in local communities;
>
> use new planting (and encourage natural regeneration) to restore abandoned or damaged land, provide for recreation, enhance the landscape in general and reduce the visual impact of new development; and
>
> use native tree species and local provenance for new planting.

small woodlands for use in the farming system, such as hedges and copses, for soil control measures or for sporting purposes; and

other woodlands, such as ornamental plantations or arboreta.

Case Study 17 shows how forestry policy can support Category V objectives.

The management of forests in Protected Landscapes could be assisted through the work of the Forest Stewardship Council (FSC)[2]. This is an international non-profit organisation that supports environmentally appropriate, socially beneficial, and economically viable management of forests. The FSC's international labelling scheme for forest products is a credible guarantee that the product comes from a well-managed forest. FSC also supports the development of national and local standards to encourage forest stewardship at the local level, backed up by guidelines for regional certification standards. Forests managed to FSC standards could be expected to make a contribution to Category V objectives.

---

[2] For more information on the FSC, see http://www.fscoax.org/

CASE STUDY 17.
Former Champion Lands, Vermont, USA – encouraging sustainability in forest management

Maine, New Hampshire and Vermont are three of the most forested of the United States. Owned by private companies, many forests in the region have long been managed primarily for forest products, while allowing public access. In the past decade, many of these forests have been put up for sale, raising questions about their future use and management. Recent sales of large tracts have included record-setting conservation easements to limit development, maintain productive forestry and secure recreational access (an easement is a restriction of allowable land uses made with the consent of the landowner, encumbering the deed of the property, and legally binding on all future landowners.)

One such transaction involved the purchase by a coalition of public and non-governmental organisations of approximately 132,000 acres (53,000ha) in north-eastern Vermont from Champion International (a paper products company). Encumbered by two easements for conservation and public access purposes, nearly two-thirds was resold to another private timber company, while the balance was further divided into a new state-owned wildlife management area (WMA) and an addition to the Conte National Fish and Wildlife Refuge. The WMA and refuge protect and enhance natural values, while allowing compatible public recreational access. Many activities, (e.g. hiking, cross-country skiing, hunting, trapping, fishing, boating, snowmobiling, cycling, riding and swimming), will be allowed in the WMA under a detailed management plan developed through a public process. Rights of access for these activities are secured on the private lands except where there are active forestry operations. Productive forestry is not only allowed but required on the private lands, but must be performed in accordance with a forest management plan approved by the Vermont Land Trust, a conservation NGO.

While not formally designated a Protected Landscape, the management frameworks on the former Champion lands represent an innovative approach to sustainable use of the area while conserving key natural values.

Source: Brent Mitchell

5.3.7 Fisheries

Category V protected areas will often include human communities whose livelihoods are wholly or partly dependent on freshwater or marine fisheries. Co-operation with the fishing industry is essential at every stage in the planning and management of the area. This is the case whether fishing is small-scale and community-based, large-scale and industrialised, or sport fishing for tourists. In regard to fisheries in protected seascapes, much of the general advice on sustainable resource management in and near marine protected areas is relevant (e.g. Kelleher, 1999, and Salm and Clark, 2000) and is not repeated here. However, one recent innovation that managers should be alive to is the Marine Stewardship Council (MSC)[3]. This is an independent, global, non-profit organisation, which aims to reverse the decline in the world's fisheries by harnessing consumer purchasing power. It has developed an environmental standard for sustainable and

---

[3] For more information on the MSC, see http://www/msc/org

well-managed fisheries which could be promoted for fisheries in protected seascapes: association with the MSC product label would reward environmentally responsible fishery management and practices.

5.4 Policies relating to land use planning

As lived-in landscapes, with a resident human population and often with appreciably-sized human settlements, most Category V protected areas will quite properly host a variety of economic and other activities. From time to time, these will require the replacement, construction or expansion of structures of many kinds, and significant changes in the use made of land. Such forms of development are therefore, in principle, entirely appropriate within Protected Landscapes, even though they would normally be permitted only under exceptional circumstances in other kinds of protected areas.

However, not all forms of economic development will be acceptable. Moreover, all significant structures or building operations, and all significant changes of land use, should be subject to control through some system of land use planning. This is needed so as to screen out what is not appropriate, and ensure that what is allowed is well designed and managed, and in keeping with the needs of the area.

5.4.1 Land use plans and controls

The form that such plans and controls will take, and the way in which they are operated, will depend very much on national or sub-national arrangements for land use planning, since these will normally determine how such matters are dealt with within the country's Protected Landscapes. However, some broad principles can be established for land use planning within Category V protected areas – see **Guidelines** below (Box 16).

Box 16. Guidelines for land use planning in relation to Category V protected areas (adapted from IUCN, 1994a)

General principles:

1. The system of land use planning should provide both:

   Plans, which are long-term frameworks for directing and stimulating development, changes in land use, provision of infrastructure etc. They should address the social and economic needs of those living in and using the area within its environmental capacity.

   Controls and incentives relating to changes in land use, construction etc.;

2. Any national system should apply more stringent procedures and/or policies within Protected Landscapes to accommodate their special needs (e.g. in respect of EIAs);

3. Land use planning should be operated in the public interest, and private interests should not be permitted to prejudice the wider public interest in the proper use of land and the protection of Category V protected areas;

4. While decisions may be taken by elected representatives, they should have access to professional advice; and

5. Planning should be open to public scrutiny and comment.

Cont.

Box 16. *Guidelines* for land use planning in relation to Category V protected areas (adapted from IUCN, 1994a) (cont.)

Land use plans as they apply to protected landscapes should reflect their special needs. In particular they should:

1. Cover all the Category V protected area in one plan, which may also include a buffer zone around and may extend over a wider area;

2. Seek to promote the objectives of the designated protected area;

3. Provide a robust framework for the operation of site-by-site controls;

4. Promote the interdependence of the protected area and the economy and life of local people, to the benefit of both;

5. Encourage private and public initiative that is in accordance with land use policies of the protected area;

6. Ensure that strong land use policies exist for all sectors – agriculture, forestry, fishing, tourism, urban development, transport, energy, minerals, waste management etc. – and that all these help to safeguard the special qualities of the protected landscape;

7. Involve the examination of alternative strategies for development and assess their respective environmental impact on the Category V protected area; and

8. Be themselves subject to a system of appraising their environmental, economic and social impact.

Individual development proposals that may significantly affect the protected landscape (whether within it or outside it) should be subject to a control system, with environmental assessment (EA) as necessary, which should:

1. Prescribe the activities which should come within the scope of control;

2. Always be applied if a preliminary screening indicates a possible threat to the protected area;

3. Cover the economic and social benefits and costs as well as the physical impacts;

4. Not only consider mitigating measures but also alternative means of meeting the claimed need, including the option of not proceeding at all, and the environmental impact of these options;

5. Always be undertaken before the project commences;

6. Allow for three possibilities: unconditional permission, conditional permission and refusal;

7. Require monitoring if approval is given, and corrective and enforcement action to ensure full compliance with conditions;

8. Allow for full public participation;

9. Require that any detailed EA be undertaken independently from the interest promoting the project; and

10. Be carried out in the public domain, with the results being published.

5.4.2 Zoning in land use plans

Land use plans will normally need to contain a set of geographically-based policies for different parts – or zones – of the Protected Landscape. Zoning policies of this kind will indicate what forms of building, land use change etc. will be acceptable in which parts of the designated area. Some areas may be zoned for a concentration of tourism development for example, or for the expansion of a settlement; policies in other zones will be much more restrictive. It will be found much easier to make such zonal policies 'stick' if the authorities operating the control system are not obliged to pay compensation for a refusal of permission. On the other hand, restrictions imposed without compensation will cause resentment unless there is a high level of public understanding and acceptance of the purposes of the protected area. As an alternative to, or complementing, zoning policies, another approach is criteria-based decision-making, under which all economic development is screened for its environmental and other impact. This then provides the basis for granting consent, or for rejection.

5.4.3 Proposals for small- and large-scale development

Given the very wide range of possible forms of land use development that might occur within a Category V protected area, it is difficult to establish general policies for universal application. However, some general guidance can be offered in relation to a) small-scale development projects (such as individual houses, small recreational schemes, local agricultural and forestry infrastructure, local social provision), and b) proposals for large-scale development (such as a new mine, a large dam, a new highway or a defence establishment).

In respect of **small-scale proposals**, the key test is whether the scheme will enhance the objectives of the protected area and meets the requirements of sustainability – whether it is "fit for the place and fit for the purpose". Box 17 offers some guidelines of this kind.

Box 17. *Guidelines* on the suitability of small-scale development in Category V protected areas

The following check list may help to establish the suitability of small-scale projects for inclusion within a Category V protected area (only a few of the factors listed below will be relevant to most schemes):

Environmental factors:

Scale: does the project conform to the general scale of other buildings and that of the landscape around?

Design: is the design sympathetic to its surroundings in term of its environmental impact?

Materials: are these of local origin, and used in a way that reflects traditional construction techniques?

Landscaping: has thought been given to the planting of trees and shrubs, to accommodate the building in the landscaping?

Cont.

Box 17. *Guidelines* **on the suitability of small-scale development in Category V protected areas (cont.)**

Off-setting benefits: has the potential to gain compensating benefits through the development, e.g. new wildlife habitat, been considered?

Location: is the location appropriate in relation to other buildings, servicing etc? are there better alternative sites?

Technologies and resource consumption: is the scheme designed to minimise use of resources (water, energy, waste, sewage, effluent, noise, light etc.)? has thought been given to using low impact technologies (either modern or traditional)?

Green practices: will the managers of the scheme follow green purchasing, use biodegradable products, seek to minimise use of private transport etc.?

Social factors:

Relationship with community: has the scheme got the support of local people?

Impact on the community: will the scheme cause an unacceptable rate of social change, threatening coherence of local communities or swamping their interests?

Impact on cultural traditions: Will the scheme support or undermine cultural traditions that identify the community, e.g. social space, circulation patterns?

Support for community: will the project underpin the community and meet its needs (e.g. for affordable housing, education or shops)?

Diversity: will the project support a diverse social community (young and old, men and women, rich and poor, various ethnic groups, and various skills and professions)?

Economic factors:

Resource users: does the project support sustainable resource use in the area, e.g. in farming or forestry? Does it deplete non-renewable resources?

Employment: will the project employ local people and use local skills?

Produce: will the project make a demand for local goods and products, especially those produced in sustainable manner?

Servicing: will the scheme make reasonable demands on public services, e.g. water and transport, which must be paid for locally?

In general, **large-scale developments** are not appropriate within a Protected Landscape on the grounds of environmental impact and their incongruous character and scale. However resisting such proposals may not be easy, especially when it is argued that they meet a national need. Some suggested guidelines are offered below (Box 18) to help determine if a particular activity is acceptable within a Category V protected area or should be resisted as far as possible.

Box 18. *Guidelines* for determining the acceptability of large-scale development in Category V protected areas

The following check list – to be applied sequentially – may help to establish if a large-scale development should be accepted within a Category V protected area:

- Establish **environmental impact** through a thorough EA, preferably along lines agreed with stakeholders, and document this. This includes arrangements for monitoring operations and safeguards over such matters as (i) pollution, where there should be an effective monitoring and compliance system, and (ii) in the case of extractive industries, credible plans and secured funding for restoration and after-use treatment to remove the threat of polluted land or water. If, as a result, it appears that the development would fail to meet, or undermine, the purposes of the designated area, resist it;

- Establish if the project really serves an over-riding **national need** and is in the public interest – if it fails to meet this test, argue for its rejection;

- Determine if there is an **alternative way** of meeting the expressed need, either by (i) a different type of scheme (e.g. energy conservation can be an alternative to new generating capacity), or (ii) a different location or route outside the area – if so, argue for this alternative;

- If the scheme passes the above tests, mitigating or compensating measures should be adopted as a condition of its approval.

There is a wealth of experience in many countries in operating land use planning systems in sensitive environments. Case study 18 draws on the experience of the UK national parks: despite their name, these are in fact Category V protected areas. Case study 19 is a more site-specific example from Brazil of how land use planning has been used for conservation purposes.

CASE STUDY 18.
Land use planning in the UK system of national parks

All land in the UK, including the national parks, is covered by comprehensive land use planning legislation, dating from 1947. All significant building developments etc., or changes in land use, are controlled by the local planning authority (LPA), which has to prepare a development plan for its area. In England and Wales (and so far in Scotland) the national park authority (NPA) is the LPA (see also Box 2).

At the national level, policy advice on land use planning is provided by central government through formal guidance. This guidance advises that...."*major development should not take place in the National Parks....save in exceptional circumstances...proposals must be subject to the most rigorous examination.*"

Development Plans are prepared to cover all national parks in the UK, either by the NPA alone or jointly with the local authority. Plans include both strategic policies for land use and development, and much more detailed policies reflecting local needs and circumstances. Development plans, which normally have a 15-year horizon and are reviewed every 5 years, are usually adopted after a public inquiry.

Cont.

CASE STUDY 18.
Land use planning in the UK system of national parks (cont.)

Once adopted, the plans guide the nature and location of development that is appropriate in the park. Implementation is mainly achieved through "development control", that is the detailed system by which approval is sought for building, land use change etc. Permission may be granted, refused or approved conditionally. There is a right of appeal against the NPA's decision.

The National Park Management Plan is not formally part of the land use system but it does provide a local framework for development plan and control policies.

Source: Mike Beresford

CASE STUDY 19.
Ilha Comprida, Sao Paulo State, Brazil – land use plan to protect biodiversity

The Iguape-Cananeia Estuarine Lagoon Complex – a Category V protected area since 1987 – is one of the most productive natural marine nurseries in the world, thanks to a barrier island, Ilha Comprida (Long Island) which measures 70km by 3km. The island is also important for its genetic material and as a stopping point for migratory birds. The area has rich and diverse fauna and vegetation types (including mangroves). Ecosystems, including naturally flooded areas, sandbanks and dunes, are naturally dynamic, but are also fragile and vulnerable to urban pressures. Some traditional fishing communities survive, but much of the area is not suitable for urban occupation.

Speculative urbanisation began in the 1950s, resulting in three planned series of lots. To control this, the Ilha Comprida Environmental Protection Area (ICEPA) was established in 1987, in the context of a regional coastal plan, co-ordinated by the State government. A zoning plan was made in 1989. After the Ilha Comprida became a municipality in 1992, action was taken to implement this plan. A working group was created in 1997 to develop a local proposal, technically supported by the state Secretariat for the Environment. This limits urban development to 30% of the ICEPA, creates a wildlife zone and maintains the area's regional conservation role. This has required the transfer of building rights and the municipality has agreed to take building lots in lieu of tax. This proposal was agreed to in 1999, after several public meetings. The result is that the island's economic viability has been maintained and the heritage of the area has been protected – all through a participatory process.

Source: Marilia Britto de Moraes

5.5 Policies relating to environmental protection and conservation

Most Category V protected areas are beautiful and invoke a positive response among visitors and residents alike. Many contain dramatic views, spectacular wildlife and historic buildings. Moreover, these areas often contain assets with intangible values, expressed in the associations that people have with them. Thus the landscapes of Category V protected areas are important in themselves but are also of great economic value, as the foundation for a successful tourist industry. Sustaining this landscape heritage is therefore vital. This section deals with the policies needed to achieve that.

5.5.1 Protection of the environment

The underlying quality of the environment is vital to the survival of the landscape. Freshwater resources, the marine environment, soils and air need to be carefully managed, and protected against over-exploitation and pollution; and ecological processes, from nutrient recycling to seasonal river flooding, need to be safeguarded. In this respect, of course, protected landscapes are no different from any other places, but there is an important point to be made about co-ordination of policies. It is likely that several public agencies will be involved in programmes of environmental protection (government bodies responsible for water supply, soil protection and pollution control, for example). As far as possible, the Protected Landscape agency should aim to co-ordinate the policies and programmes of these other agencies working within the area: for example to safeguard or restore soils in zones of agricultural importance, to protect watersheds or to conserve the quality of freshwater lakes. While it may be difficult to achieve full co-ordination where legislation is weak and institutional co-operation is poorly developed, the minimum requirement is good communication with the bodies responsible. Even better is an inter-institutional commission or similar body to co-ordinate environmental management. This should ensure a shared understanding in the key fields of forward planning, day-to-day operations and emergency action.

5.5.2 Conservation of scenic values

While landscape is emphatically more than scenery, it does matter how things look. In particular, the management of change within a Category V protected area should help ensure that the scenery retains its integrity, and that the cultural components of it maintain their authenticity. These terms – integrity and authenticity – are used in the Operational Guidelines for the World Heritage Convention; an adapted version of these has relevance to the scenery of Protected Landscapes as well, see Box 19.

Box 19. Integrity and authenticity as they apply to the scenery of Category V protected areas (adapted from UNESCO, 2002)

The scenery of a Protected Landscape has integrity when its natural and cultural components are whole and intact. This requires that the area:

   includes all elements necessary to express its importance;

   is of adequate size to ensure the complete representation of the features and processes which convey the landscape's significance; and

   is not adversely affected by development and/or neglect.

   The cultural components of the scenery of a Protected Landscape have authenticity when the scenic values are truthfully and credibly expressed through a variety of attributes including:

   form and design;

   materials and substance;

   use and function;

   traditions; and

   techniques and management systems.

Protection of scenic values in Protected Landscapes is not about protecting the scenery 'in aspic' against all change, but about ensuring that any change that does take place meets these general tests of integrity and authenticity. Policies relating to the conservation of scenic values will therefore broadly be of two kinds:

- those designed to exclude the wrong kind of developments – i.e. those that would compromise the integrity or authenticity of the scene;
- those designed to encourage the right kinds of development – i.e. those that are in line with, or strengthen the integrity or authenticity of the scene.

In practice, it will usually be best to protect and enhance scenery through other policy areas, rather than treating scenery as a policy area in its own right. The most relevant policies to scenic quality are those relating to:

- resource users like agriculture and forestry, that have a major impact on the appearance of the protected landscape (Section 5. 3 above);
- the operation of land use control policies (Section 5.4 above); and
- the protection of natural and historic values (see below).

5.5.3 The conservation of nature and biodiversity

Most Protected Landscapes are important for biodiversity because of the continued existence of traditional forms of land use that support biological diversity. This arises because low intensity land use systems very often:

- allow remnant wild places (e.g. natural woodlands) to survive within areas that are used productively;
- 'mimic' natural conditions, thereby creating man-made biodiversity-rich habitats (e.g. domestic animals that graze so as to create grasslands, and rice paddies that create wetland systems); and
- involve greater genetic diversity within domesticated animals and cultivated crops (see 5.3.5 above).

Moreover, many such areas are also important because of the part that they play in the appreciation of the importance of nature to societies around the world, for example:

- many landscapes are valued as an expression of a specific spiritual relationship between people and the rest of nature;
- they are often outstandingly beautiful – though in contrast with most other protected areas, the aesthetic values usually derive as much from the contrast, and/or interaction, *between* the works of nature and those of humankind as from the intrinsic quality of the natural features themselves; and
- they inform present generations about significant past relationships between humanity and nature.

Against this background, it is helpful to assess Protected Landscapes for their natural values and biodiversity in particular, using the checklist in Box 20.

In the light of this analysis, it will be clear that Category V protected areas call for a rather different approach to the conservation of biodiversity to that used in many other types of protected area. Biodiversity conservation in other kinds of protected areas generally involves protecting nature **against** the pressures of people. While this policy will also have a potential application in parts of Category V protected areas – such as

---

Box 20. A checklist for the natural qualities and biodiversity of Category V protected areas (after Lennon (ed.), in print)

Managers of Protected Landscapes may find it helpful in assessing the significance of the area to conservation of nature and biodiversity to consider these questions:

Conservation of natural and semi-natural ecosystems, and of wild species of fauna and flora: Does the protected landscape:

   - contribute to the protection of natural ecosystems (e.g. by providing for the protection of watershed forests, or marine or freshwater systems);
   - help protect wild species of fauna or flora;
   - help protect genetic diversity within wild species; and
   - create semi-natural habitats of great importance to biodiversity, i.e. manipulated ecosystems with well-structured and functional interactions between its living components?

Conservation of biodiversity within farming systems: Are there traditional farming systems which:

   - sustain a wide range of varieties of domesticated livestock; and
   - sustain a wide range of varieties of cultivated crops, such as cereals, fruit or root vegetables?

Sustainable land (and water) use: Do land use practices in the area:

   - respect the productive capability of land;
   - conserve the quality and quantity of soil;
   - manage and safeguard water quality;
   - manage streams and rivers so as to reduce damaging floods and run-off;
   - maintain plant cover;
   - restore vegetation, soils and sources of water; and
   - protect marine environments?

Enhancement of scenic beauty: Does the area have important scenic qualities, deriving as much from the contrast and/or interaction between the works of nature and humanity as from the intrinsic quality of the natural features themselves?

Ex situ **collections**: Are there important herbaria, botanical gardens and arboreta, or collections of fauna in the area?

Important example of humanity's inter-relationship with nature: Is the area a good example of a successful or failed relationship between a past civilisation and natural resources?

Importance to the history of science: Is the area the site of some historically significant discovery in the natural sciences?

---

nature reserves within them, which may be classified as Category Ia or IV (see Figure 2) – biodiversity protection in these areas will in general place a greater emphasis on:

   - supporting traditional land use practices that themselves sustain nature and wild-life – see photo 13;

    linking biodiversity and landscape protection;

    restoring biodiversity values that have been lost or degraded; and

    regulating those activities which degrade or erode natural values.

Box 21 expands on this by setting down suggested guidelines for the conservation of biodiversity in Category V protected areas.

Box 21. *Guidelines* for the conservation of biodiversity in Category V protected areas

Though the policies for the conservation of biodiversity will vary greatly according to the habitats and species which occur in the area, some general principles exist:

    identify all key areas for nature conservation, all endangered species and key ecological processes;

    identify the condition of, the trends in, and the threats facing key areas, endangered species and key ecological processes;

    draw up Biodiversity Action Plans which can focus on priorities and targets for conservation;

    develop programmes to address threats and targets;

    develop programmes for the restoration of habitats and species that have been destroyed or degraded (including re-introduction programmes for important species);

    develop programmes to control or eradicate invasive plant and animal species;

    develop promotional and supportive "stewardship packages" (of advice, finance etc.) for owners to help them manage biodiversity in their care;

    support traditional land use practices, especially those of farming and forestry, that help to maintain biodiversity conservation;

    develop a multi-disciplinary and integrated approach to biodiversity management;

    encourage all inhabitants, and especially primary land users (farmers, foresters, fishers etc.), to adopt a stewardship ethic, and avoid practices that threaten biodiversity;

    build on the traditions and values of the community that support nature;

    develop programmes for public education in the value of biodiversity;

    create programmes of interpretation for visitors on biodiversity;

    involve local communities in conservation programmes (including programmes for volunteers, schools etc); and

    employ, or obtain access to, the expertise needed to take the professional lead in this area.

In many Category V protected areas, the support of traditional forms of farming will be a critical part of the policy for conservation of biodiversity. Case study 20 is an example of this approach applied to the Hortobágy National Park – see photos 14 and 15.

CASE STUDY 20.
The Hortobágy National Park, Hungary – biodiversity conservation through traditional farming (see photos 14 and 15)

The Hortobágy National Park covers 82,000ha. It is a World Heritage Cultural landscape, a UNESCO Biosphere Reserve, and 30% of it is a Ramsar wetland. The area is particular important for its birds, with spectacular annual migrations of 60,000 cranes. Though listed as a Category II protected area, Hortobágy has many affinities with Category V.

Extensive areas of natural grassland/wet steppe were originally grazed by wild cattle/horses. Following human occupation, these were replaced with domesticated breeds. During the Communist period, the Hortobágy Collective State Farm farmed some of the area intensively, replacing part of the natural grassland with arable crops, and regulating waterways so as to drain the area.

Following political reforms, the Ministry of Environment took over the remnants of the former state farm. The land is now managed through the Hortobágy Nature Conservation and Gene Bank Maintaining Public Limited Company. This private company employs 125 local people and manages 12,000 ha grazing and mown grassland and 2,500ha cropland (both organic operations) within the Park. The Company has reintroduced natural grazing regimes using such traditional breeds as Hungarian Grey cattle and Racka sheep. 30 individual Przewalski's Horses occupy a core wilderness zone of 2,400ha. The Company's landholding is almost self-financing.

Traditional land use management of this kind helps native species to flourish. Also the built heritage, customs and traditions of the area have been conserved or revived. With more wildlife, the company has been able to develop eco-tourism initiatives and provides information and interpretation programmes using local guides. It manages a museum, conserves buildings (*csárda* – wayside inns with food and some accommodation), and demonstrates traditional farming skills (herding, traditional costumes, working methods). The management of Hortobágy is an outstanding example of linking biodiversity management, landscape protection and the promotion of low impact traditional land use practices.

Source: Peter Ogden

5.5.4 The conservation of the built and historic heritage

Many Protected Landscapes are rich in built and historic features: often these are integral aspects of the landscape. These may be grand monuments, such as castles, palaces, temples or churches. They may be more humble features, such as farm buildings or villages built in vernacular style. Or they may be part of a working landscape, such as structures for livestock care or grain storage, traditional forms of fish traps, boundaries like walls and hedges, or land reshaping like terracing and irrigation systems. Some features will be ancient (see photo 17) – relics from former civilisations or of past and now abandoned land use practices; others may be in use to this day, having social, cultural and economic values that are still relevant in contemporary society. Sometimes it is landscape features themselves that have historic associations, such as a battlefield (see Page *et al.*, 1998). While historic features are significant in many other kinds of protected areas, they are often almost incidental. A distinguishing characteristic of the built and historic heritage in Category V protected areas is that they are an **integral** part of the area's character, and of the reasons for its protection.

Guidance on the management of such resources within a Category V protected area is bound to be general, but Box 22 offers a starting point:

Box 22. *Guidelines* for the conservation of the built and historic heritage in Category V protected areas

The following general advice should be considered:

- it is essential first to identify the most important built heritage and/or traditional assets in the protected landscape – all action should be based on knowledge and understanding;
- identify also the contribution that these assets make to the quality of the landscape;
- establish the condition of such features;
- establish the threats that face them;
- establish the opportunities that exist to increase the protection given to such places;
- develop zone-based policies for the protection and/or restoration of the built historic heritage;
- adapt and re-use historic assets rather than replace them, wherever possible;
- for large and complex sites, draw up detailed management and conservation plans;
- promote appropriate, sensitive economic uses of historic buildings;
- support such action with programmes for public education on the value of the built and historic heritage;
- create programmes of interpretation for visitors;
- develop promotional and supportive "packages" (advice, finance etc.) for owners to help them manage heritage features in their care;
- ensure as far as possible that the traditional skills needed to protect the historic heritage are sustained, properly valued and appropriately rewarded;
- build on the traditions and values of the community that support the historic heritage;
- involve local communities in built heritage conservation programmes (including programmes for volunteers, schools etc); and
- employ, or obtain access to, the expertise needed to take the professional lead in this area.

An example of the conservation of a nationally-important historic feature is given in Case Study 21; this also shows the potential for a well-managed linear historic feature to be the core of a landscape conservation initiative.

CASE STUDY 21.
Rideau Canal Corridor, Canada – historic feature as the core of a Category V protected area

The Rideau Canal, both national historic site and Canadian heritage river, is the central feature of a 202km evolved continuing cultural landscape in eastern Ontario. Constructed through remote wilderness as part of Britain's defensive strategy for Canada (1826–1832), the canal joined natural lakes and rivers of two major watersheds into a navigable waterway and opened the Rideau corridor to settlement and economic development. The built heritage of the canal – a sophisticated adaptation of British canal-building technology in engineering works, defensive structures, lock stations and water management – retains a high degree of authenticity. Along the corridor, settlement patterns of villages and farms and land use activities from agriculture to lumbering, which shaped the 19th-century rural landscape, have evolved in response to the natural and cultural environments.

Today the canal is an active recreational waterway that remains intact and fully operational along its original course. The layered linear landscape still speaks remarkably to human interaction with the natural environment. Woodlands, wetlands and diverse habitats of the corridor ecosystem are valued for their historic connection as well as their ecological importance.

The canal's Commemorative Integrity Statement, which focuses on historic values but recognises a significant environmental stewardship role for the canal, guides the Management Plan and Parks Canada's promotion of sustainable tourism and on-going protection in the area. Challenges in protecting the natural and cultural heritage of the canal corridor include influencing municipal planning policies in 26 adjacent heritage communities and minimising the impact of land use activities on extensive privately owned shorelands.

Source: Susan Buggey

5.5.5 Conservation of contemporary cultural/spiritual values[4]

As lived-in landscapes, most Category V protected areas have important living cultural values, which are of contemporary significance. Also, individual historic assets often have great contemporary relevance, such as an ancient religious structure or a site that still plays a pivotal role in society. These present-day values may be apparent in the way that people look upon the landscape – for some communities, mainly indigenous peoples, their relationship with the landscape may embody many of their spiritual beliefs and much of their cultural identity, including their relationship with the rest of the natural world and with their ancestors. To many communities, mountains have a particular significance which it would be wise to recognise and build on in developing management policies (Bernbaum, 1997). Religious landscapes which are often carefully protected by local communities, have important natural and cultural values. Even among communities that no longer live so close to nature, the role of landscape in cultural identity is often strong, and is recorded in popular tradition (song, dance and legend) and in the arts (painting, literature, music and poetry). In many places these values are held so strongly by the community, that they provide an effective *de facto* form of protection.

---

[4] For further advice, consult the web site of WCPA's task force on Non-Material Values of Protected Areas, see http://wcpa.iucn.org/theme/values/values.html

Here again the distinctive nature of Category V protected areas is apparent. Whereas many protected areas of all kinds are important to local people for their cultural associations, this is usually related in some way to the place of the *natural* world in people's lives. But many Category V protected areas contain landscapes that bear a strong imprint of the work of past human generations. Examples are terrace cultivation or irrigation systems that represent many hundreds of years of perseverance in difficult conditions. These often have an added significance when they are the creation of the ancestors of the very people who live there and work the land to this day along similar lines. In such cases, the present generation may well have a true stewardship role: inheriting, caring for, and passing on a land whose physical features, and the cultural traditions associated with it, testify to that struggle.

Guidelines for the management policies for such culturally-specific issues must be very generalised, but nonetheless some broad rules can be proposed – see Box 23.

Box 23. *Guidelines* for the protection of contemporary cultural/spiritual values

In managing a Protected Landscape, regard should be had to these considerations:

- Establish the cultural and spiritual values that people perceive in the landscape by consulting a) local people (particularly 'elders' among them), b) local and other groups interested in such matters, and c) experts, such as anthropologists, ethnographers, cultural and art historians;
- Identify in particular those beliefs, values etc. which are linked to the protection of the present day landscape and could thus help to reinforce its conservation;
- Identify in particular those places etc. that are especially important (e.g. as sacred sites, spiritual routes or as treasured viewpoints) and ensure they are protected;
- Make it clear that traditional values are respected and will be defended;
- Seek recognition of these values through appropriate management policies;
- Involve local people in the development and implementation of management (e.g. particular traditions, associations and behaviours may not be officially recorded and an established working relationship with the community will ensure that they are identified in a timely and non-confrontational manner);
- Mobilise local communities to work to protect key sites; and
- Consider the potential for interpretation programmes for visitors on cultural and spiritual values, and involve local people in delivering information to them where appropriate.

Two case studies (22 and 23) illustrate how peoples in different parts of the world look upon their landscape and suggest the kind of management response that this calls for.

CASE STUDY 22.
Sierra Nevada de Santa Marta, Colombia

The Sierra Nevada de Santa Marta is a Biosphere Reserve. It is an isolated mountain, reaching 5,775m but only 42km from the Caribbean coast. It covers 17,000km^2, contains all the climatic zones of South America from coast to snowfields, and is a key area for biodiversity. It is the source of 36 rivers and contains two national parks and two indigenous reservations. The welfare of the 1.5 million people who depend upon the area for water is threatened by extensive deforestation.

The area is also of great archaeological and cultural importance. Thousands of years of settlement culminated in the pre-conquest Tairona civilisation. Present day indigenous culture is rich: three groups, the Kogi, Sanka and Ijka (or Arhuacos), believe they must protect their homelands which were entrusted to them by the "Mother of the Universe". They are though under pressure from outside settlers.

An NGO, the Fundación Pro-Sierra Nevada de Santa Marta (FPSN), works for the conservation of the natural and cultural heritage of the area through improved living conditions of local people. Prominent among stakeholders are the indigenous groups. In 1991, FPSN prepared a conservation strategy and subsequently a Sustainable Development Plan for the Sierra Nevada. Pilot schemes to implement these were initiated in 1997 and a programme for the whole area adopted for 1999–2006. A central theme of this activity is to strengthen the cultural identity and protect the rights of indigenous groups, and at the same time to conserve and restore the natural resources upon which these groups' cultural identity depends. Capacity building to reinforce the social fabric among indigenous and peasant communities is also a priority as well as the value of indigenous knowledge.

Source: Guillermo Rodriguez

CASE STUDY 23.
Sahyoue/Edacho, Canada – a sacred landscape

Two peninsulas on Great Bear Lake in Canada's Northwest Territories, Sahyoue/ Edacho (Grizzly Bear Mountain and Scented Grass Hills) are sacred sites that the Sahtu Dene people have used since time immemorial. The relationship between culture and landscape is a key component of Sahtu Dene identity as a people. Thus:

- cosmological, geographic, ecological, cultural, and spiritual worlds are intimately intertwined in a holistic universe;
- natural resources of the open boreal forest are sustained by traditional land use and lifestyles based on hunting, trapping, fishing, camping, plant-gathering and knowing the land;
- traditional narratives tell of appropriate land use, of relations with animals, and of ancestral spirit beings whose heroic actions made the earth safer; also of dangers and proper conduct;
- places act as mnemonic devices for recalling names and narratives that instruct the people from generation to generation in living with this complex landscape;

Cont.

CASE STUDY 23.
Sahyoue/Edacho, Canada – a sacred landscape (cont.)

■ to ensure behaviour respectful of the spirits, many places should not be visited, and visitors should travel only with a knowledgeable guide.

Protection of sacred sites and telling of associated stories are essential to the continuity of Sahtu Dene culture and livelihood. Designation as a national historic site (1996) recognises the values of the landscape but carries no legal protection. The Deline Dene Band Council and community of Deline, supported by local and national organisations, sought interim land withdrawal through federal authorities. Granted in accordance with the Northwest Territories Protected Areas Strategy (2001), it provides protection while multiple stakeholders work towards long-term safeguards and management consistent with ecological and cultural values.

Source: Susan Buggey

5.6 Policies relating to tourism, public awareness, education, information and interpretation

Category V protected areas are to be managed "mainly for landscape/seascape protection and recreation" (IUCN, 1994). Policies for sustainable recreation, tourism and public enjoyment are therefore important features in the management of most, if not all, Protected Landscapes (Section 5.6.1). Planning for tourism is closely linked to awareness raising, education, public information and interpretation (Section 5.6.2).

5.6.1 Sustainable tourism

IUCN has recently published advice on tourism in all kinds of protected areas (Eagles *et al.*, 2002). It contains much detailed guidance on the topic. In several places, it identifies the special needs and characteristics of tourism in Category V protected areas. The most important point is that, in Category V protected areas, provision for recreation and tourism is usually **fully integrated** into the local economy and social circumstances rather than being just a "park service". This is why, in Category V protected areas:

■ it might sometimes be appropriate to accommodate some carefully regulated general tourism, e.g. a well-designed resort-type development of appropriate scale, whereas in most protected areas the focus would be on ecotourism (ibid p.23);

■ it would often be appropriate to provide accommodation and other forms of servicing for tourists **within** the designated areas so as to bring economic benefits to local communities (ibid p.69), whereas these might be excluded from most protected areas;

■ many facilities that serve local needs in Category V protected areas – e.g. the road network, footpaths, shops and places to eat and drink – will be shared with visitors, so there is scope to develop visitor facilities to help meet the needs of the local community; and

■ many partnerships will need to be built with the private, voluntary and community sectors for the provision of services to visitors in Category V protected areas;

these should be developed on an equal footing rather than through concessions, as would be the norm in most Category II protected areas.

But if recreation and tourism are important parts of the economy of many Category V protected areas, their development should nonetheless follow the principles of sustainability. This relates both to new tourism development and to established provision which needs to be realigned along more sustainable lines. The tourism that takes place in Category V protected areas should have integrated environmental, economic and social aims – see Box 24, which draws on the work of EUROPARC Federation in Europe (2001). The same report has also been drawn on in preparing the guidelines recommended in Box 25 to ensure that capital tourism projects in Category V protected areas are sustainable.

Box 24. The aims of sustainable tourism in Category V protected areas (from EUROPARC Federation, 2001, p.22).

Environmental aims:

- conservation over the long term; and
- better knowledge and awareness of conservation among local people and visitors.

Social aims

- visitor satisfaction and enjoyment;
- improved living standards and skills among local people;
- demonstration of alternative to "mass" and package tourism, and promotion of sustainable tourism everywhere;
- making sustainable tourism part of local and national culture; and
- enabling all sectors of society to have the chance to enjoy the protected area.

Economic aims

- improvement of the local and national economies;
- provision of local business and employment opportunities; and
- generation of increased revenue to maintain the protected area.

Box 25. *Guidelines* for sustainable tourism in Category V protected areas (adapted from EUROPARC Federation, 2001, p. 22).

Protected Landscape planners and managers should develop policies for tourism and recreation through the following steps:

- Develop clear conservation aims, based on discussion and agreement about the place of sustainable tourism with other key partners;
- Compile an inventory of natural and cultural features of tourism use and potential, and then analyse this information;
- Work in partnership with local people, the tourism sector, and other local and regional organisations;

Cont.

> **Box 25.** *Guidelines* **for sustainable tourism in Category V protected areas (adapted from EUROPARC Federation, 2001, p.22) (cont.)**
>
> Identify the values and image on which to base sustainable tourism;
>
> Assess the carrying capacity of different parts of the area and set environmental standards that must be maintained;
>
> Survey and analyse tourist markets and visitors' needs and expectations;
>
> Give guidance on tourism activities which are compatible with the protected area, and which are not;
>
> Propose new tourism "products" to be developed, including those for educational tourism;
>
> Assess the environmental impacts of proposals;
>
> Specify the management measures required, such as zoning and channelling, linked to interpretation and education;
>
> Propose traffic management and development of sustainable transport systems;
>
> Set out a communications and promotional strategy to promote the image of the protected area, new "products" and management techniques;
>
> Establish a programme of monitoring the protected area and its use by visitors, and for revision of the plans for tourism development to ensure that tourism maintains environmental standards;
>
> Assess resource needs and sources, including provision for training;
>
> Capture a proportion of the tourism-generated income to reinvest in the maintenance of the environment;
>
> Always develop policies and new initiatives in consultation with those most directly affected; and
>
> Implement the plans for tourism.

The managers of Category V protected areas may be faced with proposals for new tourism development. If the aims in Box 24 are to be achieved, such schemes should be assessed according to the general guidance set out in Box 18 above, and the specific advice in Box 26.

> **Box 26.** *Guidelines* **for capital tourism projects in Category V protected areas**
>
> *Within Protected Landscapes all significant capital projects for tourism provision should:*
>
> be undertaken only after an Environmental Assessment has established the social, economic and environmental impact and any necessary mitigation measures have been adopted;
>
> be located where the negative impact on the landscape is minimal and positive benefits for the local community and economy are maximised;
>
> be planned and designed to have the minimum negative impact upon the landscape (including scenery, biodiversity and built and historic heritage) and where possible enhance it;
>
> Cont.

Box 26. *Guidelines* for capital tourism projects in Category V protected areas (cont.)

be designed to respect and support local cultural values;

be built with indigenous materials, or properly "sourced" materials which guarantee that they come from sustainable systems;

be generally operated to minimise the wasteful use of natural resources (e.g. water, energy, waste, sewage, effluent, noise, light etc.), and maximise the reuse and recycling of all resources used (e.g. 'green purchasing', minimal use of private cars), and specifically incorporate low impact technologies (e.g. energy saving systems, waste water recycling);

be managed so that it is subject to sustainability standard setting, periodic review and operational adjustment so as to ensure that impacts remain minimal;

incorporate programmes to enhance the understanding of staff, visitors and local residents about environmental sustainability in general, and the specific scenic, ecological, social, cultural and historical values of the protected landscape;

be planned and operated in close liaison with the local community;

be run so as to ensure that local people can get real and lasting benefits (jobs, income, education) from the economic activity generated; and

include, if possible, a means for part of the profits of the operation to be ploughed back into the conservation of the protected landscape which in effect sustains the tourism enterprise.

Case studies 24 and 25 describe efforts to cater for visitors in Category V protected areas and some of the potential problems that may well have to be faced.

CASE STUDY 24.
Laikipia/Samburu Heartland, Kenya – wildlife-based and tourism-financed community development

The vast landscapes of the extensive Laikipia plateau, in North Central parts of Kenya, contain a great diversity of wildlife which thrives in the semi-desert conditions. The pastoral Samburu people herd their goats, sheep, cattle and camels in the shadow of Mt. Kenya, a crucial source of water for humans and animals alike. Laikipia-Samburu is the focus of the Africa Wildlife Foundation's (AWF's) effort to develop wildlife-related businesses aimed at conserving natural resources and improving the economic well-being of local communities.

The AWF Wildlife Economic research programme identifies the ways in which landowners might use their holdings for wildlife conservation and preservation, tourism and other activities. The communities and ranch owners get advice on managing wildlife businesses. A programme on Participatory Business advises and works closely with community groups to generate ideas for natural resource business. Laikipia beekeepers are trained and assisted with the technology to meet

Cont.

CASE STUDY 24.
Laikipia/Samburu Heartland, Kenya – wildlife-based and tourism-financed community development (cont.)

international guidelines for harvesting and processing honey for export. The establishment of Samburu cultural homesteads is another wildlife-related business that benefits the local people while encouraging conservation. Overall, the number of wildlife killed in the area has declined significantly since the local people have been able to develop alternative economic opportunities from tourism.

Source: Bob Wishitemi

CASE STUDY 25.
Jiuzhaigou Valley Scenic and Historic Area, China – the pressures of tourism (see photo 1)

Jiuzhaigou Valley, Sichuan Province, China covers 72,000ha and is listed as a Category V protected area. In 1992, it was inscribed on the World Heritage list as a natural site, notably for its beautiful scenery, including remarkable karstic (tufa) waterfalls and travertine lakes. It is also important for bird life, forest habitat for such endangered species as the Giant Panda and the cultural values of the Tibetan communities living in the valley.

The area is very attractive to tourists. In 1998 it had 300,000 visitors, and pressures from tourism will increase as improved transport connections are made with the rest of China. While all major hotel development has taken place outside the park and valley, tourist pressures create significant problems in the absence of effective management. Tourists' minibuses and some cars using the narrow roads cause localised pollution, visual disturbance and erosion. Visitor behaviour disturbs wildlife and destroys the sense of great beauty. Local Tibetan settlements have benefited economically from tourism but are vulnerable to over-commercialised development with little regard for scenic values or cultural traditions. Several international missions to Jiuzhaigou have suggested a strategy based on controlling vehicular numbers entering the valley, substituting a park-and-ride alternative (at least at peak time), training staff to interpret natural values to visitors, and generally seeking to raise visitor understanding and behaviour. Radical measures are needed to deal with congestion if the benefits of tourism are not to be outweighed by environmental costs.

Source: Adrian Phillips

5.6.2 Public awareness, education, information and interpretation

There is a close connection between tourism and the enjoyment of Category V protected areas and the related issues of public awareness, education, information and interpretation. In particular, one of the principal benefits of tourism in protected areas is that it should lead to better knowledge and awareness of conservation of natural and cultural values among visitors and local people (Box 25).

Thus the 'targets' for education are both those who live in the area and those who visit it. But their needs are rather different:

▢ *For those living in the area, the need is to foster an awareness of their landscape and culture, and to sustain, re-awaken or develop a pride in their significance.* Under the impact of alien cultural influences, local people may sometimes undervalue the importance of their own culture and traditions. This in turn can undermine culturally-related land use and other practices which are critical to the survival of the landscape heritage. Without denying people access to the benefits of modern living, it is desirable to institute educational programmes that aim to revive cultural traditions, arts and crafts. These can help to reinforce community pride and identity, and provide a source of additional income. Such efforts should be considered both at the school level (through courses and materials which are integrated where appropriate into national curricula) and with adults through programmes of community learning and training.

▢ *For visitors, the need is to foster an appreciation of why the area, its landscape and its people are important, and to develop a sense of respect for its significance.* Here the advice already set out by IUCN in relation to tourism and protected areas (Eagles *et al.*, 2002) is especially relevant. This stresses that both potential and existing park visitors require information, varying from simple facts about the location of the protected area and opening times, fees for facilities, to much more complex interpretation of cultural history and local ecology. Visitors need access to information about the area that they are visiting before, during and sometimes after their visit. As their understanding of the area grows, visitors will show more curiosity about its natural environment and history, about the culture of people living in it, and about the role of visitors. This is the demand to which inter-pretation should respond. The result of well-planned interpretation should be a more fulfilling visitor experience for thousands of people.

Protected Landscape agencies should develop policies for public awareness, edu-cation, information and interpretation. Guidelines for the content of such policies are given in Box 27.

Box 27. *Guidelines* for policies for public awareness, education, information and interpretation

Policies should:

▢ address the needs of the local people, the visitors and the managers;

▢ be based both on the unique characteristics of the landscapes, and of the links between nature and people, past and present, tangible and intangible values;

▢ be designed to raise awareness of, and a sense of responsibility towards the landscape;

▢ be delivered through a range of mechanisms, involving face-to-face contact (e.g. through protected area staff), technology and audiovisual techniques (e.g. use of the internet), and printed matter (e.g. leaflets);

▢ use a range of facilities, from visitor centres to self-guided trails;

▢ be explicit on the criteria regarding the location of visitor and interpretation centres etc.;

▢ wherever possible, involve local people themselves as guides, interpreters etc.; and

▢ be brought together in an interpretative/educational plan.

An example of the application of such guidelines is given in Case study 26 below.

CASE STUDY 26.
Tarangire/Manyara Heartland, Tanzania – education for conservation

The landscape of the Tarangire/Manyara region is composed mainly of savannah, lakes, swamps and flood plains. It includes Lake Manyara National Park, the Marang Forest, a large area of the Maasai steppe and some small urban areas. Much of the land outside the national parks is used for ranching and/or agriculture. It is in this Heartland that Tanzania National Parks and the Africa Wildlife Foundation (AWF) have pioneered community-based conservation, encouraging Park authorities and local people to address wildlife issues together through education and extension programmes.

The communities have been trained and empowered to manage their resources by AWF and the Park authorities. Many joint activities in the field of education and training have been implemented, such as training courses and technical meetings for managers and local people, and school exchanges have been encouraged. All training programmes for stakeholders are participatory in nature. Information has been spread and public awareness raised through various communication mechanisms: audiovisual aids, press releases, books, brochures and newsletters, on-site demonstrations and exhibitions etc., and particular awareness campaigns have been mounted. Information has been targeted at key groups of local people. The aim has been to develop a common understanding among different stakeholders and to build support for conservation throughout the area. This vital locally-focused effort is in addition to interpretation services offered by the Park's staff for visitors.

Source: Bob Wishitemi

5.7 Additional policies to promote sustainable resource use

One of the principles for the management of Category V protected areas is that they should be 'models of sustainability', with a view to developing lessons for wider application (Box 11). What this means is that governments should regard, and managers should promote Protected Landscapes as 'exemplars' of sustainable development. This is particularly so in relation to the use of natural resources in sectors like farming, forestry and tourism (see above).

But the idea can be taken further: Category V protected areas can also exemplify high standards of sustainability in fields relating to resource use more generally. A general approach which is often advocated is to minimise the environmental impact of resource use by **reducing** the amount of resources used for a particular purpose in the first place, **re-using** resources wherever possible, and **re-cycling** them when this is not. Box 28 suggests how these principles might be applied to energy generation and conservation, structures, waste management and water supply. Promoting sustainable approaches in this way would improve the environmental quality of Protected Landscapes, and the quality of life of those who live or work in the area, or visit it for recreation purposes.

At present, such ideas are still in their infancy in Protected Landscape management. They call for greater influence over many arms of public policy and private action than can normally be secured at present. It is therefore premature to propose guidelines. However, a few countries are beginning to explore some of these ideas (for example, government funds are available to support innovative schemes of this kind within the national parks of England and Wales). Further, the suggestions in Box 28 point towards the development of an important new role for Category V protected areas, in which they could become pioneers in society's search for more sustainable futures.

Box 28. Sustainable approaches to energy, structures, waste and water in Category V protected areas

Policies for the sustainable use of resources within Category V protected areas, notably energy, structures, waste and water, could cover such matters as:

Energy: aim at a 'carbon neutral' target for the area, at least in the longer term. This requires:

- a switch in energy generation from fossil fuels to renewable energy (e.g. solar, wind, wave, tidal, geothermal, energy crops and other forms of biomass energy), with perhaps some generating capacity of this kind in the area, providing the environmental character of the area is not compromised (see Boxes 17 and 18);

- energy conservation (e.g. encouraging designers and owners of properties to set and meet high standards of insulation, and generally promote energy efficiency in buildings);

- climate change mitigation measures (e.g. tree planting);

- discouragement of fossil fuel-powered vehicles, and encouragement of those using alternative low- or no-carbon technologies.

Structures: aim at a minimum resource use strategy. This calls for:

- designing new buildings etc. so that, in both their construction and operation, resource use demands are minimised;

- re-using redundant existing buildings wherever possible;

- recycling materials from demolished buildings and other structures as far as possible.

Waste: aim at waste minimisation. This requires:

- environmentally-sound waste collection and disposal methods;

- the adoption of state-of-the-art standards to minimise resource use and waste minimisation;

- encouraging the recycling of biodegradable and other waste by all residents, shopkeepers, businesses and commercial enterprises, farmers, builders and other potential waste generators in the area;

- minimising the transport of waste to disposal sites, and generally making the waste creator responsible for its disposal.

Water: aim at the highest standards of management: This includes:

- integrated management of river basins using "green" techniques of flood minimisation (e.g. removing artificial drainage in catchments) and flood control (e.g. allowing natural flooding to occur rather than combating it);

- support for innovative domestic and commercial techniques to reduce water consumption and increase recycling; and

- recovering a proper level of reimbursement from towns downstream that use water resources whose quality and quantity depends on the protection of watersheds in protected landscapes.

---

6. Management of Category V protected areas: Processes and plans

6.1 Introduction

The management of Category V protected areas requires appropriate processes and plans. They are so closely linked that it makes sense to deal with them together.

This chapter recommends the adoption of management processes that are participatory, iterative, adaptive and flexible. **Participatory** means that the community affected should play a central role in management planning and implementation (Section 6.2). **Iterative** means that management is conceived of as a cyclical, not a linear exercise, with feedback loops. **Adaptive** means that learning is built into the process and management adapts to lessons learnt. **Flexible** means that management planning has to take account of a huge variety of national and local circumstances – and any advice given here must therefore not be regarded as prescriptive but as general guidance for adaptation to particular circumstances.

This chapter puts the Management Plan at the heart of the management process. It briefly describes the status, scope, form and content of the plan in Section 6.3 (cross referenced to Annex 2), suggests a participatory method for its preparation (6.4), and describes the systems of monitoring and evaluation that are needed and should lead to adaptive management (Section 6.5). Finally it identifies the connections between the Management Plan and other strategies and plans (Section 6.6).

6.2 Community involvement and participation

As noted above (Section 5.1), local people should be a principal focus in policies for the management of Category V protected areas. But they are also an essential part of the *process* of management. Thus management of Protected Landscapes is not only largely undertaken *for* the local community (i.e. applied through **policies** within the protected area), but it is also undertaken *with* and *through* them (i.e. through the **processes** used to manage the area). In particular, local people have a vital role to play in shaping the Management Plan (Section 6.3 below and Annex 2).

6.2.1 A continuum of levels of involvement

The different options for involving local people and other stakeholders can be placed on a continuum, from very limited involvement to a wholesale transfer of responsibility – see Figure 11.

Fig. 11 The Participation Continuum (after Borrini-Feyerabend G., ed. 1997)[1]

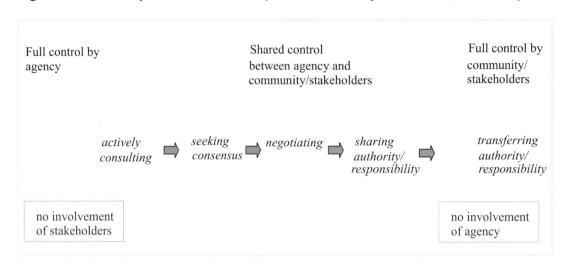

It is possible to achieve a degree of management of a Category V protected area at any point along this continuum, and of course to vary the extent of participation according to the matter under consideration. There is no 'right' place to be on the spectrum: different approaches will be needed in different situations. However, experience from many countries suggests that the prospects for enduring conservation and successful partnerships with stakeholders, and especially with the local community, are better if the style of management lies towards the right-hand end of the above scale. This is when stakeholders become active partners in management of the area under an arrangement known as 'co-management'. But moving along the continuum to the right – which means that more and more powers and responsibilities are given away or shared, has significant resource and other implications for the managing authority. Few authorities are yet willing or able to abdicate entirely, as indicated at the right hand extremity.

6.2.2 Co-management

The term 'co-management' embraces a number of particular techniques that have been developed to promote the successful involvement of stakeholders in protected area management. These present guidelines to Category V protected areas cannot do justice to the amount of detailed work that has been undertaken to develop the principles and practice of co-management. However, Box 29 defines the term and briefly identifies its key features.

---

[1] These ideas derive from Sherry Arnstein's 'ladder' of citizen participation (1969).

Box 29. Co-management of protected areas (after Borrini-Feyerabend *et al.*, 2000)

Note: **Co-management** *has also been called participatory, collaborative, joint, mixed, multi-party and round-table management. There may be subtle differences but all these concepts would fall within this definition of co-management:*

"A situation in which two or more social actors negotiate, define and guarantee amongst themselves a fair sharing of the management functions, entitlements and responsibilities for a given territory, area or set of natural resources".

As thus defined, co-management:

- is a pluralist approach to the management of natural resources;
- aims to achieve environmental protection, ecologically sustainable use of natural resources, and the equitable sharing of resource-related benefits and responsibilities;
- is a political and cultural process, seeking "democracy" in the management of natural resources;
- requires some basic conditions to succeed, such as full access to information, the freedom and capacity to organise, freedom to express needs and concerns, a non-discriminatory social environment, and recognition of the equal status and validity of all views;
- takes time, can be frustrating for all involved, and is not straightforward; but
- is an expression of a mature society in which it is recognised that there are many different sources of knowledge and wisdom about the management of natural resources (and also many potentially negative options for the environment and development).

Applying co-management approaches as a means of achieving full stakeholder involvement in protected areas is always complex and sensitive; in lived-in, working landscapes it will be an even greater challenge. Nonetheless, whilst the approach to each site has to adapt to local conditions, there are some basic Guidelines for stakeholder involvement in Category V protected areas, see Box 30.

Box 30. *Guidelines* for stakeholder involvement in Category V protected area management (after Borrini-Feyerabend G., (ed.) 1997)

At the outset, protected area agencies should all clarify the reason for stakeholder involvement, so as to guide their own approach and to inform others. They should then:

First, identify and inform stakeholders by:

Drawing up an inventory of actual and potential stakeholders;

Undertaking an analysis of stakeholders and their needs;

Carrying out an information campaign to inform stakeholders;

Providing a public relations service to interact with stakeholders; and

Undertaking discussions with stakeholders through open dialogue.

Cont.

Box 30. *Guidelines* **for stakeholder involvement in Category V protected area management (after Borrini-Feyerabend G., ed. 1997) (cont.)**

Then build on the capacities of stakeholders and build long-term partnerships with them by:

- Promoting discussion about the protected area within each group;

- Helping the stakeholder groups to organise themselves;

- Setting up meetings etc. to build bridges between stakeholders;

- Exchanging experience with successful participatory-based conservation initiatives;

- Strengthening local institutions for sustainable resource management;

- Setting up an Advisory Forum, Conservation Council, or similar body, for key stakeholders to advise management agency and for communication between stakeholders (its scope may extend beyond conservation issues);

- Setting up a mechanism or institution for conflict management, negotiation, arbitration etc.;

- Training of staff to improve their people-based skills; and

- Promoting a legal framework that favours collaboration with stakeholders.

Finally, consider taking further steps to involve the stakeholders in management by:

- Supporting conservation initiatives by the community themselves;

- Underpinning community-based initiatives, such as local volunteers for conservation, and school's and women's conservation groups;

- Undertaking participatory action research, in which stakeholders play a key role in shaping conservation policy for the area;

- Drawing up an agreement for some form of collaborative management with stakeholders;

- Creating an institution to develop a management agreement and a management plan for the area – unlike an Advisory Forum or Council (see above), this would have the power to make decisions;

- Devolving the initiative to local institutions where there is the capacity to manage the area; and

- Setting up systems for participatory monitoring and evaluation, so that the stakeholders can themselves assess effectiveness.

6.3 The Management Plan: Status, scope, form and content[2]

6.3.1 The status of the Management Plan

In principle, the management of all protected areas should be guided by a plan; indeed it is the key to successful management. The Management Plan for a Category V protected areas is a high profile, flagship document which sets out the overall strategy for the Protected Landscape. It therefore represents the major policy document and should provide both a lead and a framework for other plans and programmes relating to the area.

The plan should aim to motivate partners and make a clear case for funding from a wide range of sources. It is therefore essential that it should attract a wide readership, including not only the "partner" organisations, but also the many agencies and groups with an interest in the area. It is not simply an internal organisational plan for the management authority, but one for the area, aimed at co-ordinating the efforts of all the stakeholders who can influence the management effort.

The Management Plan should therefore be an inclusive document, aiming at a high degree of collaborative management between the management agency, its main partners, and key interest groups. It should clearly specify and guarantee respective functions, rights and responsibilities.

6.3.2 The scope, form and content of the Management Plan

Note: A fuller explanation of the scope, form and content of the Management Plan is given in Annex 2.

The contents of management plans for Category V protected areas will vary greatly. Plans for part of a Small Island Developing State, a rice growing area in South East Asia or an ancient farmed landscape in Europe will obviously place the emphasis on very different issues. Further, the contents of plans will reflect legal and institutional differences between countries. Nonetheless, at a certain level of generality, there are common themes. In particular, all management plans should provide clear long-term visions, which are to be realised through programmes of management action. A suggested way of presenting these is set out in Annex 2.

6.4 The Management Plan: Preparation

The process of preparing the Management Plan is as important as the plan itself. Indeed, it is the preparation process that will provide the opportunities to develop and maintain relationships with key partners, interest groups, individuals, stakeholders and other agencies whose support will be required to implement the policies in the final Management Plan. It also provides opportunities to manage conflicts between interest groups. The process of preparing the plan therefore largely determines its eventual success.

---

[2] IUCN proposes to publish general advice on Management Plans for Protected Areas in this Guidelines series during 2003.

6.4.1 The Management Plan Cycle

The Management Plan does not sit alone. There will be other strategies and plans in existence at a "higher" level that will need to be taken account of in the preparatory process, and others that will flow from the Management Plan. These are dealt with in Section 6.6.

Normally the preparation of the Management Plan will follow the designation of the Category V protected area. However, it is possible to reverse the order. In the case of the French Regional Nature Parks, for example, the Management Plan is drawn up **before** designation, which makes it possible for the local community to learn about the significance of the protected landscape before it happens and helps in drawing the right boundaries. Whatever sequence is followed, an iterative cycle is required – see Figure 12.

Fig. 12 The Management Plan cycle (cross-referenced to subsequent sections)

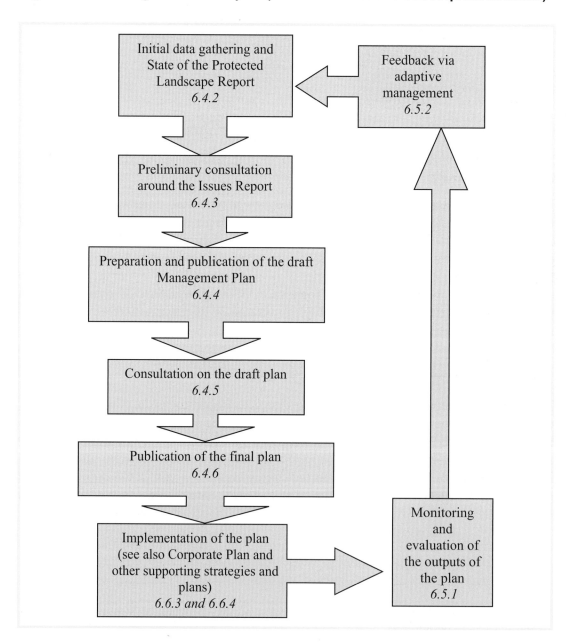

6.4.2 Initial information gathering and preparation

The basis of all good management plans is good intelligence. Thus the initial task of those preparing the plan is to gather and review available data about the area which is relevant to the aims of the plan – that is the natural and cultural resources of the area, the people who have an interest in it (i.e. the stakeholders), and the trends, pressures and opportunities which it faces. Since local people are a source of much information of this kind, public involvement should start even at this early stage. From this review, an initial report on the '**State of the Protected Landscape**' may be prepared.

A "State of the Protected Landscape" Report is a useful tool of Category V management. It provides statements of the condition of the environmental, natural and cultural assets of the area, and lists the factors that impact on it. It also covers relevant social and economic factors relating to the well-being of the local community. If such a report is prepared, it should be done as part of the Management Plan process: thus it should be published before the Management Plan, and help to formulate the **Issues Report** *(see below)*. Preparing this report may reveal gaps in information; further work should then be put in place to fill these.

The base line data in the State of the Protected Landscape reports are an important input to the management planning exercise. Through periodic updating and the collection of trend data, the reports provide an objective means of setting targets, of monitoring progress towards them, and of assessing the effectiveness of the policies of the Management Plan. Updating is most easily done electronically, and can be closely linked to the regular monitoring and review of the Management Plan itself. Some Protected Landscape management agencies revisit this report annually, and use it to monitor action (and inaction!), issues and trends (see section 6.5 below).

6.4.3 Preliminary consultation

Such a preliminary review is needed to embark on the second stage, which directly involves the community affected. At this stage, the protected area agency should:

i)   inform stakeholders of its intention to prepare a management plan;

ii) explain why a plan is necessary;

iii) introduce the implications of the exercise, such as the issues that may need to be addressed by the plan;

iv) explain how stakeholders can participate in the process; and

v)   solicit views on the plan and what it should contain.

The basis for such a preliminary consultation is usually a single document, often called the "Issues Report". It may be necessary to vary the precise form of the document to the target audience, but it should always be short, concise and easily readable, and conveyed to stakeholders in a variety of socially appropriate means. Generally, local communities are not used to being consulted and some may have difficulty in following even the clearest and most readable of documents. In many parts of the world, indeed, poor levels of literacy or the use of indigenous languages will require other approaches to consultation. The onus is on the agency to reach out to the community, but at the same time it will need to use its judgement as to how representative stakeholder groups really are. It should hold meetings with groups and individuals to make sure that the issues are well understood. This may be through seminars, informal discussions, 'village drama', school plays, 'road shows' - whatever it takes to get people involved. Local elders, head teachers and other community leaders will advise the agency on the most appropriate way to engage the public. Getting the strategy right and budgeting for it properly are vital, or the whole participation exercise runs the risk of wasting a great deal of time and money, and will fail in its objective.

As a rough guide, some three months might be set aside for this exercise. While this might need adjustment in certain circumstances, (for example, more time may be needed where a complex negotiation process with indigenous groups is required), it is important not to allow the process of preliminary consultation to 'drag out' as this can generate cynicism among the groups concerned.

6.4.4 Preparation and publication of the draft Management Plan

The feedback from this preliminary stage will enable the Protected Landscape agency to prepare the draft plan. The time taken to carry out this work might be around nine months, and will involve further data gathering and consultations to clarify areas of uncertainty. At the end of this process a publication will be available for wide distribution and further consultation. The suggested content of this is described in Annex 2, but at this draft stage it may be appropriate to include certain options upon which further public views are sought.

6.4.5 Consultation on the draft Management Plan

The aim of this stage is to ensure that all stakeholders' views are heard and taken account of while the plan is still in draft form. Wherever the management style is located on the scale in Figure 11, wide public consultation is always essential. Similar processes may be used to those employed at the earlier preliminary consultation phase (6.4.3). It is particularly important that Part 1 of the plan (see Annex 2), and notably the vision, is widely debated while in draft. The aim is to ensure that the final document reflects the values and issues generated through the participation programme. The objective is to produce a wide sense of ownership of the plan among all the parties. Box 31 suggests guidelines on how this process of consultation should be conducted:

Box 31. *Guidelines* for consultation on the draft Management Plan

It is essential that the consultation processes create confidence among all stakeholders. This requires that the agency:

  identify all the stakeholders (see Box 29);

  approach all of them on the basis of equality and transparency;

  produce materials that are informative, clear and user-friendly;

  use a variety of culturally appropriate means to seek views;

  emphasise the draft nature of proposals;

  be ready to revisit any proposal;

  keep a complete and documented record of all comments, and log all contacts;

Cont.

> **Box 31.** **_Guidelines_** **for consultation on the draft Management Plan (cont.)**
>
> ▫ ensure that all requests for meetings, materials etc. are responded to promptly;
>
> ▫ make sure that every view has been considered, whether it is adopted or not;
>
> ▫ allow time so that people do not feel rushed by the process, but not so much that they lose interest;
>
> ▫ engage in further consultation if changes in the plan are envisaged that will affect other stakeholders than those seeking these changes;
>
> ▫ feedback the results of consultation to all who commented; and
>
> ▫ above all treat the stakeholders as essential partners in the conservation of the protected landscape, not obstacles.

6.4.6 Publication of the Management Plan

In light of the outcome of this exercise, which may take up to six months, the final version of the management plan can be prepared. A further six months should normally be allowed for this last task, making in all about two years from start to finish.

6.5 Monitoring, evaluation and adaptive management

6.5.1 Monitoring and evaluation

Monitoring and evaluation, and the incorporation of the results of this through adaptive management, are essential aspects of management planning for protected areas – an iterative process, not a linear one (see Figure 12). It is vital therefore that proposed methods for monitoring and evaluating the effectiveness of the plan are contained in it. For each policy area, there should be targets and measures to judge performance against which progress can be assessed (see also Annex 2).

A number of issues need to considered in developing agreed performance indicators. Thus data on the condition of the environment need to be collected by regular updating of the "State of the Protected Landscape" report (see Section 6.4.2): this is a 'reality check'. It is also important to establish current trends that affect the environment and local communities, and any changes that are likely to affect management.

On the basis of this, it will be possible to develop indicators to assess the progress made in implementing the policies in the management plan and the impacts of this, and to assess the performance of the agency itself.

What distinguishes monitoring in Category V protected areas from that in other protected areas is not so much the process as the scope. As explained in Chapter 5, policies in such areas will include those relating to social and economic objectives, notably those which concern the local communities' relationship with the landscape, as well as environmental objectives (for further advice, see Hockings *et al.*, 2000).

6.5.2 Adaptive management

The main purpose of monitoring and review is to feed back the lessons learnt into the management of the Category V protected area. This requires that management is adaptive, and that managers "learn by doing". Adaptive management may be thought of both as a **style** of management – responsive, reflective, flexible – and as a **technique**, calling for periodic review and updating of policy in the light of experience. It is relevant to the management of all protected areas but especially that of Category V protected areas because it helps to gain and keep the trust of the local community and stakeholders generally.

The results of monitoring and review should therefore be an adjustment in management practices. It may involve no more than a small adaptation of a policy for one sector. However, after a period of at least five years, but not more than ten, the results should be used to undertake a more wide ranging review of the management plan as a whole, including a new cycle of stakeholder participation.

6.6   Programmes, plans etc. that support the Management Plan

6.6.1 A "sea" of other plans

Though the Management Plan is the core document for a Category V protected area, in most cases it will be only one of a number of related plans, programmes etc. affecting the area (see Figure 13). These are of several kinds:

- "higher level" and sectoral plans, e.g. those drawn up by national, regional and local bodies, affecting the area (6.6.2);

- plans etc. for issues that may need to be developed in greater detail than is possible in the Management Plan (6.6.3); and

- plans, audits etc. that help the agency to manage its own operations effectively (6.6.4).

Fig. 13   The relationship between the Management Plan and other plans and strategies (omitting feedback loops)

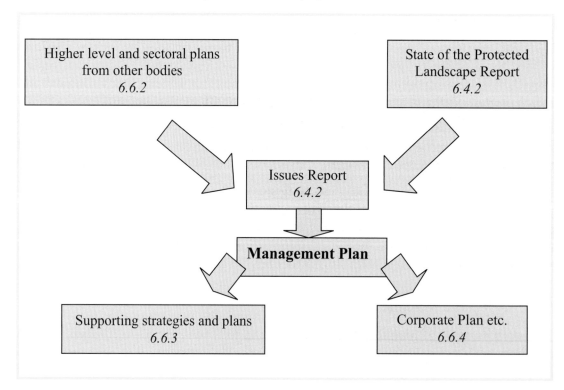

6.6.2 Higher level and sectoral plans etc.

The powers available to management agencies for Protected Landscapes (Section 7.1) vary greatly. Typically they include: some direct responsibilities, e.g. for landscape and nature protection and visitor management; other areas in which they have a considerable influence, e.g. land use planning; and other fields again where they have very little or no influence (e.g. health, housing and education for local people). Some Category V agencies do have powers to control development themselves; others have only a limited say in what gets built and where. But no management agency is a law unto itself, and all must take account of plans made at the national and regional level that may affect the area under their responsibility.

As a general rule, the effectiveness of management – and in particular of conservation – is increased when the agency has greater powers, especially those of land use planning. But whatever the arrangement, it is likely that the Management Plan for the Category V protected area will be subordinate to national and regional priorities, and that it will be complemented by other strategies and plans for such matters as:

- regional development;
- land use;
- agriculture;
- tourism; and
- transport.

When the responsibility for preparing and implementing these plans does not rest with the agency itself, it should do all in its power to seek the co-operation of the body that is responsible. Clearly an enabling legal framework will help here (see Section 3.2). Ideally, the responsible bodies should recognise and embody the principles of protected landscapes planning (Chapter 3) in their own strategies and plans. Moreover, the objectives set out in the particular Management Plan should be embedded as far as possible in the scope and detail of these other documents. At very least, these higher level, or sectoral plans should recognise the significance of the area and the need for special policies that protect its qualities.

6.6.3 Supporting strategies etc. for issues dealt with in greater detail than in the Management Plan

The Management Plan for some Category V protected areas may need to be supplemented by other supporting strategies for issues that cannot be dealt with fully in that plan itself. The topics covered in such supplementary planning or similar documents will vary greatly from area to area. They may:

- cover an issue where there is a need for very detailed, scientifically-justified action, such as those needed to save a number of endangered species or an endangered habitat;
- deal with a topic, such as the marketing of a farm product or a grant programme for owners of historic buildings, that is of interest to one specific group of stakeholders;
- be focused on a particular part of the whole area, such as the coastline, which faces very distinct problems; or

relate to a theme that needs to be developed as a stand alone document to catch public attention or for marketing purposes, such as an interpretative strategy that requires support from the private, public and voluntary sectors, or a plan for the development of a network of trails.

The status of such documents can vary. Thus some (such as Design Guides) are advisory; some may record formal or informal agreements between parties; and some may be declarations of commitment to the purposes of the area made by stakeholder groups. The key points about all such supplementary plans etc. are that: they should always be based on, and derive from the Management Plan itself; and their preparation should involve the same kind of consultation and stakeholder participation as is required for that plan.

6.6.4 The Corporate Plan and other plans, audits etc. that help the agency to manage its own operations effectively

As noted above, the Management Plan should aim to co-ordinate and influence the activities of **all** those groups whose activities impact on the Protected Landscape, and not just the protected area agency itself. However, there may also be a need to develop plans etc. that are specifically for the operations of the agency itself, and are designed to ensure that the agency is well managed and appropriately organised to undertake the tasks expected of it in the Management Plan. Examples are an annual budget and work plan, which will authorise commitment of finance and staff time to particular projects; and a set of internal performance indicators by which to measure the efficiency and effectiveness of the agency's operations.

Budgets, work plans and performance indicators may be incorporated within a **Corporate Plan**, which is a regularly updated business plan for the agency as a means of explaining to the public how effectively the organisation is fulfilling its responsibilities. It should explain how the agency operates, set out its objectives and priorities, and measure its performance in relation to these objectives. For partners and stakeholders, it provides a framework for involvement and investment.

When a Corporate Plan is prepared, it should clearly flow from the Management Plan. It will establish a performance framework for the agency responsible for the protected landscape, and its preparation will present a significant challenge. It will be invaluable in:

- assessing the performance of the agency itself against the purposes of the Management Plan;

- demonstrating to donor agencies that the management agency is seeking to achieve best value for money, and that the protected landscape is being well managed;

- helping the agency's partners and key stakeholders, local communities and visitors to understand how the agency works, and providing scope to comment on policy objectives;

- guiding the agency's staff in implementing, reviewing and updating the Management Plan.

7. Management of Category V protected areas: Means

7.1 Administration/management Agency

As the 1994 guidance on Category V protected areas makes clear, there is no one 'right' organisational arrangement or agency for all such areas. Instead these will vary from country to country, taking account of national and local conditions. Some possible models are illustrated in Box 32.

Box 32. Some organisational structures used for Category V protected areas

A wide range of administrative structures can be found for the management of Category V protected areas e.g.:

- managed as a national or regional service – Hungarian National Park Directorate;
- managed as a special service of local **and** central government – e.g. UK National Parks (see Case Study 2);
- managed as a normal service of local government – e.g. UK Areas of Outstanding Natural Beauty;
- managed primarily as an alliance of regional and local interests – e.g. the French Regional Nature Parks (see Case Study 10);
- managed jointly by the central government/National Park Authority and local community organisation – e.g. Buffer Zones of Nepal (see Case Study 3);
- managed through an *ad hoc* task force etc. – e.g. Philippine Rice Terraces – (see Case Study 4);
- management led by an NGO – e.g. Saint Lucia National Trust (see Case Study 11);
- management led by the private sector – e.g. El Paramo de Guerrero (Colombia);
- management led by a local community – e.g. South Pacific Community Conservation Areas (see Case Study 7).

So rather than recommending one model, Box 33 gives guidelines on the characteristics that make for a successful managing body.

Box 33. *Guidelines* **for a managing body for a Category V protected area**

A successful managing body for a Category V protected area will need to be:

- properly empowered to do the job: this goes back to the legal basis; unless this is sound, the managing body will raise false expectations and lack credibility;
- furnished with adequate resources of staff and finance: see Sections 7.2 and 7.3 below;
- kept properly informed about environmental, social and economic conditions: the 'State of the Protected Landscape' report and its updating are intended to do that;
- seen to be enjoying the support of the Government: this is needed to ensure that the legal powers are there, to help it secure the funds it needs and to ensure that all branches of government are obliged to take the importance of the Protected Landscape into account in their own plans and operations;
- capable of building partnerships with local and central government: in most Category V protected areas important responsibilities are shared between local government (e.g. in services like housing or local roads) and central/provincial government (e.g. environmental protection), and so the agency must be able to work with both;
- capable of working with all stakeholders: as noted throughout, the greater the degree of genuine stakeholder involvement, the more likely it is that the protected area will enjoy the support of local people;
- committed to building the capacity of the local community to manage the Protected Landscape. Beyond stakeholder participation in shaping policies for the area, there lies the bigger prize of increasingly involving local people themselves in the running of the protected area. As noted above, they are often the true 'managers' of such areas and the official management should do all it can to build the capacity of the local community to carry this task;
- readily accountable for its actions: accountability may be achieved in various ways. This can be done formally through direct election of a protected area managing board by the people within the area, but – maybe more importantly – through: transparent and equitable ways of working; through a collaborative, communicative and consultative style; through a strong commitment to adaptive management; and through genuine stakeholder participation;
- supported by credible consultative institutions: public (and NGO) management boards need to develop formal and informal means to consult with the local community and other stakeholders. A Conservation Council or similar body is one way of involving a wide range of stakeholders in a consultative capacity (see Box 30); and
- with access to good scientific and technical advice: this may be secured from the staff, through a formal or informal expert advisory board, by links with local universities and/or in other ways.

7.2 The staff

As in all protected areas, the staff employed in the service of a Category V protected area are critical to its success. Ideally the team should be:

- led by a senior person with strong leadership skills, and with wide experience in conservation, visitor management or rural development issues;

- include a range of professional backgrounds relating to: environmental protection (ecology, biology, landscape, archaeology etc), economic development and social concerns;

- strong on people-related skills, like collaborative working, negotiation, conflict management and communication;

- strong on resource-use and land-based skills, like agriculture, forestry and fisheries;

- strong on recreation management, and working with the tourist sector;

- strong on business skills, especially in financial management and innovative funding;

- contain both field staff (e.g. rangers, community outreach people, agriculture and forest liaison staff) and office staff;

- properly supported by human resource expertise;

- backed up with good technical competence in such areas as IT, presentations and graphics; and

- supported through programmes of training and career development, appropriate to the breadth of responsibilities carried by the agency. A priority should be training in multi-disciplinary skills (e.g. ecologists who understand community participation, foresters with good communication skills, administrators with business skills).

While such a multi-disciplinary team of this kind represents the ideal, inevitably many protected landscape staff teams will be under-resourced, especially where the full potential of such designations has not yet been appreciated. However, a creative approach to partnerships can be used to reinforce the effectiveness of even small teams. In many Category V protected areas, additional help can be obtained in a number of ways – see Box 34.

Box 34. *Guidelines* for augmenting staff capacity for Category V protected areas

The following approaches should be considered as ways of adding additional capacity to a small staff team:

- seek volunteers to work in the field (e.g. as volunteer rangers) or in the office (e.g. as volunteer receptionists). Appoint a staff member to develop volunteer capacity. Recently-retired people often represent a neglected resource of potential volunteers;

- develop co-operative partnerships with local or international NGOs under which expertise is offered to the protected area over the long term;

Cont.

Box 34. *Guidelines* **for augmenting staff capacity for Category V protected areas (cont.)**

- seek sponsorship from local businesses, under which they loan professional people (e.g. accountants) for specific tasks;
- agree with the local tourist industry that they will take on a role in providing protected area information to visitors;
- involve local schools and other local institutions in caring for particular parts of the protected area with which they have a close association; and
- develop partnerships with local universities to use the Protected Landscapes as an outdoor laboratory (including dissertations by PhD and other students).

7.3 The finances

As with all protected areas, the funding of Category V protected areas represents a continuous challenge. It is certain that there will never be sufficient funds for all the tasks that need to be undertaken. Against this background, IUCN has published several pieces of guidance recently on the financing of protected areas (WCPA Economics Task Force, 1998–2000, Athanas *et al.*, 2001 and Eagles *et al.*, 2002). This identifies the various sources from which protected area managers can generate additional streams of income, such as tourists, international development assistance and business. While it is as relevant to Protected Landscapes as to other protected areas, it is not repeated here. Nonetheless, this type of protected area presents some unique challenges and opportunities.

Because Category V protected areas have a substantial local human population, there are ways in which public and private funds made available to support aspects of the local economy can also be used to achieve the aims of the Protected Landscape. Often such investment has a potential downside, since it may stimulate action that has a negative impact on the area – but with some adjustment this can be turned to a positive end. Some examples are shown in Box 35.

Box 35. *Guidelines* **for securing additional funds for Category V protected areas**

Over and above the usual range of financing that is potentially available to protected areas, there are other ways of supplementing funds in the case of Category V protected areas, e.g.

- investment in local tourism infrastructure: it may be possible to access public or private funds to support village-based or farm-based tourism (e.g. accommodation, shops, servicing) that will benefit the local economy, sometimes support the restoration of traditional buildings and help visitors to enjoy the area with minimal environmental impact;
- visitor contributions: because visitor services, such as accommodation, shopping, catering etc., are likely to be located **within** the protected area, there may be scope to develop voluntary levies (so-called 'visitor pay-back' or 'environmental premium' schemes), or to operate local tourism taxes, the proceeds of which can be earmarked for the management of the Protected Landscape;

Cont.

> **Box 35.** ***Guidelines*** **for securing additional funds for Category V protected areas (cont.)**
>
> ▢ farm and forestry grants: often farm and forestry subsidy systems work against the interests of the landscape and the environment, but there are examples (see Case Study 11) where such support is now being directed to environmental care and can thus help achieve the purposes of the Category V protected area; and
>
> ▢ "enabling development": this term describes the process whereby a permit is given to a developer to carry out some construction etc., subject to a condition that he/she makes a contribution towards the environment, for example by tree planting, or perhaps providing an endowment to finance and run a visitor centre, or donating some other land for conservation purposes. Though such deals are not without their dangers, used creatively they can bring real environmental benefits.

The generation of additional protected area-related funds and other equivalent resources in this way adds to the finances available to meet management aims. It is also a concrete demonstration of the economic value of the landscape and of the designated area. This can be expected to increase local support for the area and its objectives.

Investment which is 'captured' for the purposes of the protected area from outside the normal budget sources may or may not lead to additional funds passing through the management agency itself. If it does, then such funds must be accounted for in a transparent way. Indeed all the agency's funds should be clearly allocated in accordance with Management Plan priorities (e.g. through annual programmes and budgets), and their use monitored, accounted for and reported in line with good practice.

7.4 Information management and IT

Effective management of any protected area depends on good information. In the case of Category V protected areas, as already noted, this calls for databases on the state of the environment, the socio-economic condition of local people, and the nature and impact of any uses which affect these resources. Information of this kind will be used in the 'State of the Protected Landscape' report, underpin the management plan and form the basis of monitoring and review (Section 6.5.1).

As a matter of good practice, information **relating to the environment** which is collected in the management of the Category V protected area should:

▢ wherever possible be stored and analysed electronically;

▢ be generally regarded as in the public domain and therefore made freely available on request (subject only to a charge to reflect the time involved in meeting the request);

▢ kept regularly updated; and

▢ offered to *bona fide* researchers, universities etc, for further analyses in the public interest, and as an incentive to them to share the results of their research with others.

However, in the case of **socio-economic data**, it may be appropriate to confirm with the stakeholders that they are content to see it used in the above way: in some cases it may be culturally inappropriate, or offend conventions of privacy, to distribute it without prior agreement.

The relevance of IT to Category V protected areas extends much further. Through the Internet, it can also:

- be used to exchange good practice between various protected areas engaged in similar work, both nationally and internationally. The Category V Task Force of WCPA has developed a database for this purpose, which will be posted on the WCPA web site at www.wcpa.iucn.org;

- be used interactively as an important educational resource;

- provide up-to-date information and interpretation to anyone interested in the area, including to visitors before they come, when they do so, and afterwards; and

- provide information to the local community and other stakeholders about the area, the issues it faces, and on progress being made in its management. It may be possible to develop an interactive capacity as well, so that feedback from stake-holders can be gathered on-line.

Annexes

Annex 1

Guidelines for Category V protected areas – Extract from the Guidelines for Protected Area Management Categories (IUCN, 1994, p.22)

CATEGORY V: Protected Landscape/Seascape: protected area managed mainly for landscape/seascape conservation and recreation

Definition

Area of land, with coast and sea as appropriate, where the interaction of people and nature over time has produced an area or distinct character with significant aesthetic, ecological and/or cultural value, and often with high biological diversity. Safeguarding the integrity of this traditional interaction is vital to the protection, maintenance and evolution of such an area.

Objectives of management

- to maintain the harmonious interaction of nature and culture through the protection of landscape and/or seascape and the continuation of traditional land uses, building practices and social and cultural manifestations;

- to support lifestyles and economic activities which are in harmony with nature and the preservation of the social and cultural fabric of the communities concerned;

- to maintain the diversity of landscape and habitat, and of associated species and ecosystems;

- to eliminate where necessary, and thereafter prevent, land uses and activities which are inappropriate in scale and/or character;

- to provide opportunities for public enjoyment through recreation and tourism appropriate in type and scale to the essential qualities of the areas;

- to encourage scientific and educational activities which will contribute to the long-term well-being of resident populations and to the development of public support for the environmental protection of such areas; and

- to bring benefits to, and to contribute to the welfare of, the local community through the provision of natural products (such as forest and fisheries products) and services (such as clean water or income derived from sustainable forms of tourism).

Guidance for selection

- The area should possess a landscape and/or coastal and island seascape of high scenic quality, with diverse associated habitats, flora and fauna along with manifestations of unique or traditional land use patterns and social organisations as evidenced in human settlements and local customs, livelihoods, and beliefs.

- The area should provide opportunities for public enjoyment through recreation and tourism within its normal lifestyle and economic activities.

Organisational Responsibility
The area may be owned by a public authority, but is more likely to comprise a mosaic of private and public ownerships operating a variety of management regimes. These regimes should be subject to a degree of planning or other control and supported, where appropriate, by public funding and other incentives, to ensure that the quality of the landscape/seascape and the relevant local customs and beliefs are maintained in the long term.

Equivalent Category in 1978 System
Protected Landscape

Annex 2

Suggested scope, form and content for Management Plans for Category V protected areas

Introduction

There is no one ideal way to draw up and present a Management Plan for a protected area. However there are certain general principles and common themes, and WCPA is currently preparing guidance on protected area management planning in general which it hopes to publish in this series during 2003. Meanwhile the advice in this Annex is specifically focused on Category V protected areas. It is based on the experience of members of the Category V Task Force. It is not intended to be either prescriptive or definitive. Local circumstances will often dictate a rather different approach but it is the first time that international experience in this area has been distilled into a single set of lessons. The Task Force will be interested to receive feedback on the utility of this advice from those working in the field.

Scope

The Management Plan is the key management document for a Protected Landscape. It includes a set of aims for the Protected Landscape, strategic objectives and policies for its management. It guides the management agency in carrying out its functions and all the other organisations, groups and individuals that will partner the agency in managing the area. It has an external and an internal role. It is a plan for the Protected Landscape area, not just for the agency – see box below.

Guidelines on the scope of Management Plans (adapted from Countryside Commission 1997)

The Management Plan should:

- Set out a vision for the area, take a long-term view;
- Develop strategies and policies for the sustainable management of the protected landscape;
- Adopt sustainability as the underlying principle;
- Take account of other relevant policies that derive from the regional, national or international level;
- Integrate easily with the prevailing institutional and organisational framework of the country and region;
- Encourage innovation and leadership in conservation;
- Create a viable programme of social and economic development for the local communities and develop wider opportunities to ensure local benefits;

Cont.

Guidelines on the scope of management plans (adapted from Countryside Commission 1997) (cont.)

- Provide a framework for participation and investment so as to co-ordinate and influence the activities of all those public, private and other bodies that impact on the Protected Landscape, and not just those of the protected area agency itself;
- Develop a realistic work programme for the Protected Landscape agency and provide a co-ordinated focus for the effective management of the work programmes of its partners;
- Develop and implement policies in partnership with others;
- Concentrate on strategic issues and be concise;
- Identify priorities for action;
- Aim to reconcile conflicting human demands and interests in respect of land and natural resources;
- Be flexible enough to adapt to changing circumstances;
- Be output-oriented, identify measurable objectives and define practical and achievable targets, as a basis for monitoring, review and regular updating.

The task of preparing the Management Plan will be challenging. As stressed in the main body of these Guidelines, the essential sense of common ownership requires a substantial effort to encourage local communities, other public agencies, NGOs etc. to support and participate in the preparation of the plan, so as to build consensus for its aims and ensure that its policies are implemented.

Form and content

On the basis of experience, a two part Management Plan seems to work best:

- Part 1: an overview plan setting out a vision and long term strategy, and
- Part 2: a series of Action Plans focused on the Protected Landscape's distinctive assets and issues of opportunity or concern.

Form and content of Part 1

Part 1 should not be more than 15–20 pages, setting out the long-term view, indicating how the Protected Landscape should be managed over the next 20–25 years. Based on an Issues Report, this part of the document should establish an overall picture of how the area should be managed so as to safeguard and improve the special qualities for which it was designated. This "Vision Statement" should be supplemented by a broad statement of management principles that the agency would like to see implemented. This part of the plan aims to provide a clear sense of purpose and direction – a vision, or 'mental map', for the future of the Protected Landscape. The challenge will lie in making the vision a reality.

Profile of the area
The profile should be based on a clear, short description of the main characteristics of the Protected Landscape, identifying the particular qualities that make it special and the main issues to be faced during the next 20–25 years. It should set the area within its

international, national and regional context. It should include information relating to its natural values – wildlife, biodiversity and landscape; and its cultural and heritage values – including social and economic issues.

This profile establishes the main natural and cultural resources and key 'environmental capital or assets' of the area. It will be underpinned by a 'State of the Protected Landscape Report' (see Section 6.4.2), which will establish:

- a knowledge of the environmental stock of the Protected Landscape;
- a system which provides information for the preparation of the Management Plan and its subsequent review;
- a robust basis for monitoring change and the effectiveness of management;
- a monitoring system which identifies the key changes in the environmental stock; and
- a baseline for key management decisions.

The Vision
The Management Plan should set out a clear vision for the area. The vision statement will be developed through the participation of other agencies, key interest groups and stakeholders, particularly local communities. It will provide a long-term perspective and identify the main purposes of the management of the area for the next 20–25 years.

The statement should address the following questions:

- what are the special qualities of the natural and cultural heritage?
- what will the area be like in 25 years time?
- what will be the nature of the main changes?
- what will be the positive and negative implications of the changes?
- what will be the main benefits of change?
- what will be the major challenges of change?

The vision statement must not be too long and should:

- create a clear picture in the mind of the reader;
- address social and economic as well as environmental issues from the point of view of promoting sustainability;
- chart the general direction of change; and
- aim to be imaginative and inspire support for the Protected Landscape.

The Management Plan should adopt a long-term perspective, with a 20–25 year time horizon. But it should also include short-term or intermediate objectives, usually with a 5-year time horizon. The plan itself should be reviewed every five years. To realise the vision, the linkages between the vision statement and the strategy need to be clear and unambiguous.

The Strategy
This forms the backbone of the plan and should set out a series of aims and principles to guide the management of the Category V protected area in a more sustainable direction in future. The Strategy will:

- identify the major changes likely to take place within the area over the next 25 years;

-   state how the agency and its partners aim to respond to, and influence these changes;
-   identify key management principles (such as those in section 4.2);
-   state the priority action points;
-   identify the major problem issues; and
-   identify the main vulnerable areas within the Category V protected area.

The Strategy is a statement of fundamental principles and key policies. It will articulate the main aims, which will frame and guide the major decisions. Sustainability will be a central consideration at the strategic level.

Form and content of Part 2

Part 2 is made up of Action Plans to generate, and guide, on-the-ground action. It should be based on Part 1 and developed through a survey of stakeholder interests and the identification of opportunities therefrom. The action plans are working strategies and policies for the various issues affecting the Protected Landscape, which should set priorities for action.

This part of the plan moves from broad strategic outlines to specific policy objectives. Thus it identifies and evaluates the key management issues. It will need to anticipate changes and challenges, and it will investigate and advise how best to address them.

Action plan subject areas would normally include:

-   biodiversity conservation,
-   landscape conservation,
-   cultural heritage conservation,
-   community awareness projects,
-   community development initiatives,
-   tourism management,
-   information, interpretation and education projects,
-   forestry and fisheries management,
-   staff training,
-   budget, and
-   monitoring and evaluation.

Action plans will be developed independently over the plan period as circumstances allow. This will ensure that the Management Plan is not a 'once and for all' statement, but constantly updated, based on a continuing process in which all the partners can become involved.

Policies and objectives
The action plans in Part 2 of the Management Plan should contain policies which are clearly stated with measurable objectives. The objectives will be based on factual information, notably current trends affecting each of the policy areas, the pressures for change and lessons learnt from any previous monitoring and evaluation. They will have a number of roles: clarifying general aims into more specific and clearly definable targets; helping to define priorities; identifying the resources required for implementation; and providing the baseline information needed to monitor progress.

Setting clear policy objectives will be a challenging task. It is helpful to start by identifying a list of the main issues and then defining how these should be addressed. The key to successful objective-setting lies in identifying the main elements or special characteristics of the area and defining the linkages between them.

The words used to express policy objectives should be simple, clear and tightly structured. Loose or excessive wording results in problems later, when monitoring and measurement take place. Also, tight wording provides a better base for defining appropriate indicators.

Setting objectives and realistic targets represents a co-ordinated effort with partner agencies and interest groups, providing the opportunity to share the ownership and establish a consensus.

Objectives should be capable of change and review as circumstances dictate. For instance, new data may become available, which need to be reflected in the wording of the objectives. International events or national political or institutional change can occur at short notice and may call for new objectives to be developed to address changed circumstances.

References

Aguilar L., Castañeda I. and Salazar H., 2002. *In Search of the Lost Gender – Equity in Protected Areas*. IUCN, Absoluto. San José, Costa Rica.

Athanas A., Vorhies F., Ghersi F., Shadie P. and Shultis J., 2001. *Guidelines for Financing Protected Areas in East Asia*. IUCN, Gland, Switzerland and Cambridge, UK.

Beckmann A., 2000. *Caring for the Land – a decade of promoting landscape stewardship in Central Europe*. Environmental Partnership for Central Europe, Prague, Czech Republic.

Beltrán J. (ed.), 2000. *Indigenous and Traditional Peoples and Protected Areas: Principles, Guidelines and Case Studies*. IUCN, Gland, Switzerland and Cambridge, UK.

Bennett A.F., 1998. *Linkages in the Landscape*. IUCN, Gland, Switzerland and Cambridge, UK.

Benson J.F., and Roe M. H. (eds.), 2000. *Landscape and Sustainability*. Spon Press, London, UK.

Beresford M. and Phillips A. Protected landscapes – a conservation model for the 21st century. In *The George Wright Forum*, 2000, **17**:1.

Bernbaum E., 1997. *Sacred Mountains of the World*. University of California Press, Berkeley and Los Angeles, USA.

Borrini-Feyerabend G., Farvar T.M., Nguinguiri J.C. and Ndangang V., 2000. *Co-management of Natural Resources*. IUCN, Gland, Switzerland and Cambridge, UK.

Borrini-Feyerabend G., 1997. *Beyond Fences: Seeking Social Sustainability in Conservation* (2 vols.). IUCN, Gland, Switzerland and Cambridge, UK.

Bridgewater P., Phillips A., Green M. and Amos B., 1996. *Biosphere Reserves and the IUCN System of Protected Area Management Categories*. UNESCO, Paris, France.

Brown J., 1998 *Stewardship: an International Perspective in Environments*, **26**:1, (Special Issue: Stewardship: An International Perspective).

Brown J. and Mitchell B., 2000. The Stewardship Approach and its Relevance for Protected Landscapes. In *The George Wright Forum*, **17**:1.

Clark J., 1996. *Coastal Zone Management Handbook*. CRC/Lewis Publications, Boca Raton, Florida, USA.

Conklin H. 1980. *Ethnographic Atlas of the Ifugao: a study of environment, culture and society in Northern Luzon*. New Haven, USA.

Council of Europe, 1998. Landscapes – setting for our future lives, *Naturopa*, no. 96. Council of Europe, Strasbourg, France.

Council of Europe, 2000. *European Landscape Convention*. Council of Europe, Strasbourg, France.

Countryside Commission. 1988. *Protected Landscapes – Summary Proceedings of an International Symposium*, Countryside Commission, Cheltenham, UK.

Countryside Commission. 1992. *AONB Management Plans – Advice on their format and content*. Countryside Commission, Cheltenham, UK.

Countryside Commission and Countryside Council for Wales. 1997. *National Park Management Plans Guidance*. Countryside Commission, Cheltenham, UK.

Davey A., 1998. *National System Planning for Protected Areas*. IUCN, Gland, Switzerland and Cambridge, UK.

De Klemm C., 2000 in IUCN. *Landscape Conservation Law: Present Trends and Perspectives in International and Comparative Law*. IUCN, Gland, Switzerland and Cambridge, UK.

Diehl J. and Barrett T.S., 1988. *The Conservation Easement Handbook*. Trust for Public Land, San Francisco, CA and Land Trust Exchange, Alexandria, VA, USA.

Drost A., 2001. Establishing an International Heritage Corridor in the Champlain-Richelieu Valley. In *Conservation and Stewardship Publication* No. 2, Conservation Study Institute, Woodstock, Vermont, USA.

Eagles P.F.J., McCool S. F. and Haynes C.D., 2002. *Sustainable Tourism in Protected Areas: Guidelines for Planning and Management*. IUCN, Gland, Switzerland and Cambridge, UK.

Everhart W., 1972. *The National Park Service*. Praeger, New York, USA.

EUROPARC Federation, 2001. *Loving them to Death? – Sustainable Tourism in Europe's Nature and National Parks* (revised version). EUROPARC Federation, Grafenau, Germany.

Geoghegan T. and Renard Y., 2002. Beyond Community Involvement in Protected Area Planning and Management: Lessons from the Insular Caribbean. In *PARKS*, **12**:2. IUCN, Gland, Switzerland.

Green B., and Vos W. (eds.), 2001. *Threatened Landscapes*. Spon Press, London, UK.

Hockings M., Stolton S. and Dudley N. 2000. *Evaluating Effectiveness*: *A Framework for Assessing the Management of Protected Areas*. IUCN, Gland, Switzerland and Cambridge, UK.

ICOMOS UK, 2002. *The Cultural Landscape: Planning for Sustainable Development*. National Trust, London, UK.

IUCN, 1994. *Guidelines for Protected Area Management Categories*. IUCN, Gland, Switzerland and Cambridge, UK.

IUCN, 1994a. *Parks for Life: Action for Protected Areas in Europe*. IUCN, Gland, Switzerland and Cambridge, UK.

IUCN, 1998. *1997 United Nations List of Protected Areas*. IUCN, Gland, Switzerland and Cambridge, UK.

IUCN Commission on Environmental Law, 2000. *Landscape Conservation Law: Present Trends and Perspectives in International and Comparative Law*. IUCN, Gland, Switzerland and Cambridge, UK.

Joubert E., and Sulayem M. 1994. Management of protected areas in the Kingdom of Saudi Arabia. *Unasylva*, **176**:45, FAO, Rome, Italy.

Kelleher G., 1999. *Guidelines for Marine Protected Areas*. IUCN, Gland, Switzerland and Cambridge, UK.

Kothari A., Vania F., Das P., Christopher K. and Jha S., 1997. *Building Bridges for Conservation*. Indian Institute for Public Administration, New Delhi, India.

Lennon J. (ed.), (in print). *Management Guidelines for World Heritage Cultural Landscapes*. UNESCO, Paris, France.

Lucas P.H.C. (Bing), 1992. *Protected Landscapes for Policy-Makers and Planners.* Chapman and Hall, London, UK.

Migliorini, P. Pilot project for the development of organic agriculture and livestock in the regional parks of Tuscany, in Stolton, S., Geier B. and McNeely J. 2000. (qv).

Miller K., Chang E., and Johnson N., 2001. *Defining Common Ground for the Mesoamerican Biological Corridor.* World Resources Institute, Washington DC, USA.

Mitchell B. and Brown J., Stewardship: A Working Definition. *Environments.* **26**:1, 1998. (Special Issue: Stewardship: An International Perspective).

Mitchell N., Slaiby B. and Benedict M., 2002. Developing Partnerships with Local Communities for Conservation of Protected Areas in North America: Recent Experience in the United States and Canada. In *PARKS*, **12**:2. IUCN, Gland, Switzerland.

Mitchell N. and Buggey S., Category V Protected Landscapes in Relation to World Heritage Cultural Landscapes: Taking Advantages of Diverse Approaches. In *Conservation Study Institute et al., 2001.* Landscape Conservation – an International Working Session on the Stewardship of Protected Landscapes, Conservation Study Institute, Woodstock, Vermont, USA.

Ogden P., 2002. *Guidelines for the Sustainable Use of Agricultural land in the Protected Landscapes of the PHARE Countries.* EUROPARC, Grafenau, Germany.

Oviedo G. and Brown J., 1999. Building Alliances with Indigenous Peoples to Establish and Manage Protected Areas in Stolton S. and Dudley N. (eds), *Partnerships for Protection: New Strategies for Planning and Management of Protected Areas.* IUCN and WWF-International, Gland, Switzerland.

Page R.R., Gilbert C.A. and Dolan S.A., 1998. *A Guide to Cultural Landscape Reports: Contents, Processes and Techniques.* US National Park Service, Washington DC, USA.

Romulus G. and Lucas P.H.C., From the Caribbean to the Pacific: Community Conservation in Small Island States. *The George Wright Forum*, 2000, **17**:1.

Rossler M., World Heritage Cultural Landscapes. *The George Wright Forum*, 2000, **17**:1.

Salm R., and Clark J., 2000. *Marine and Coastal Protected Areas.* IUCN, Gland, Switzerland and Cambridge, UK.

Sandwith T., Shine C., Hamilton L. and Sheppard D., 2001. *Transboundary Protected Areas for Peace and Co-operation.* IUCN, Gland, Switzerland and Cambridge, UK.

Sarmiento F.O., Rodriguez G., Torres M., Argumedo A., Munoz M. and Rodriguez J., Andean Stewardship: Tradition Linking Nature and Culture in Protected Landscapes of the Andes. *The George Wright Forum*, 2000, **17**:1.

Stolton S., Geier B., and McNeely J., 2000. *The relationship between nature conservation, biodiversity and organic agriculture.* IFOAM, Germany.

Tuxill, J. L. and Mitchell N.J. (eds.), 2001. *Collaboration and Conservation: Lessons Learned in Areas Managed Through National Park Service Partnerships.* Conservation Study Institute, Woodstock, Vermont, USA.

Tuxill, J.L (ed.), 2000. *The Landscape of Conservation Stewardship.* Marsh-Billings-Rockefeller National Historical Park, The Woodstock Foundation, and the Conservation Study Institute, Woodstock, Vermont, USA.

UNESCO, 1999. *Operational Guidelines for the Implementation of the World Heritage Convention.* UNESCO, Paris, France.

UNESCO, 2002. Draft Revised *Operational Guidelines for the Implementation of the World Heritage Convention*. UNESCO, Paris, France.

Tilburg D. M. (ed.), 2000. *Landscapes and Sustainability – Proceedings of the European workshop on landscape assessment as a policy tool*. ECNC, Netherlands.

Weber R., Butler J. and Larson P. (eds.), 2000. *Indigenous Peoples and Conservation Organisations*. WWF/US, Washington, USA.

WCPA Economics Task Force, 1998. *Economic Values of Protected Areas – Guidelines for Protected Area Managers*. IUCN, Gland, Switzerland and Cambridge, UK.

WCPA Economics Task Force, 2000. *Financing Protected Areas – Guidelines for Protected Area Managers*. IUCN, Gland, Switzerland and Cambridge, UK.

Von Droste B., Plachter H. and Rossler M. (eds.), 1995. *Cultural Landscapes of Universal Value: Components of a Global Strategy*. Fisher Verlag, Jena, Germany.

World Conservation Monitoring Centre (WCMC), 1987. *Protected Landscapes: Experience around the World*. IUCN, Cambridge, UK.

WWF Scotland, 2001. *Stewardship of Natural Resources*. WWF Scotland, Abernethy, Scotland, UK.

Zbicz D., 2001. Global List of Complexes of Internationally Adjoining Protected Areas. In Sandwith *et al.*, (2001) – see above.